The Time at Darwin's Reef

To Pam –
Helper angel
of the finest kind!
Many thanks!
Joan A Mad
2/18/03

ETHNOGRAPHIC ALTERNATIVES BOOK SERIES

Series Editors: Carolyn Ellis & Arthur P. Bochner
Department of Communication
University of South Florida
4202 East Fowler Avenue, CIS 1040
Tampa, FL 33620-7800
Email: cellis@chuma.cas.usf.edu

About the Series: Ethnographic Alternatives emphasizes experimental writing that blurs boundaries between the social sciences and the humanities. We encourage submissions that experiment with forms of expressing concrete lived experience, including literary, poetic, auto-biographical, multi-voiced, conversational, performative, visual, critical and co-constructed representations. We seek writing that narrates local stories, ethnographic settings, dialogue, and unfolding action; that includes the author's involvement in the research process and reveals strategies for practicing reflexive fieldwork.

Current titles:
Volume 1, *Composing Ethnography: Alternative Forms of Qualitative Writing*, Carolyn Ellis and Arthur P. Bochner, editors
Volume 2, *Opportunity House: Ethnographic Stories of Mental Retardation*, Michael V. Angrosino
Volume 3, *Kaleidoscope Notes: Writing Women's Music and Organizational Culture*, Stacy Holman Jones
Volume 4, *Fiction and Social Research: By Fire or Ice*, Anna Banks and Stephen P. Banks, editors
Volume 5, *Reading Auschwitz*, Mary Lagerwey
Volume 6, *Life Online: Researching Real Experience in Virtual Space*, Annette N. Markham
Volume 7, *Writing the New Ethnography*, H. L. Goodall, Jr.
Volume 8, *Between Gay and Straight: Understanding Friendship Beyond Sexual Orientation*, Lisa Tillmann-Healy
Volume 9, *Ethnographically Speaking: Autoethnography, Literature, and Aesthetics*, Arthur P. Bochner & Carolyn Ellis, editors
Volume 10, *Karaoke Nights: An Ethnographic Rhapsody*, Rob Drew
Volume 11, *Standing Ovation: Performing Social Science Research about Cancer*, Ross Gray and Christina Sinding
Volume 12, *The Time at Darwin's Reef: Poetic Explorations in Anthropology and History*, Ivan Brady

The Time at Darwin's Reef

Poetic Explorations
in Anthropology and History

IVAN BRADY

ALTAMIRA
PRESS
A Division of
ROWMAN & LITTLEFIELD PUBLISHERS, INC.
Walnut Creek • Lanham • New York • Oxford

AltaMira Press
A Division of Rowman & Littlefield Publishers, Inc.
1630 North Main Street, #367
Walnut Creek, CA 94596
www.altamirapress.com

Rowman & Littlefield Publishers, Inc.
A Member of the Rowman & Littlefield Publishing Group
4720 Boston Way
Lanham, MD 20706

PO Box 317
Oxford
OX2 9RU, UK

British Library Cataloguing in Publication Information Available

Library of Congress Cataloging-in-Publication Data Available

ISBN 0-7591-0335-6 cloth
ISBN 0-7591-0336-4 paperback

Printed in the United States of America

⊖™ The paper used in this publication meets the minimum requirements of American
National Standard for Information Sciences—Permanence of Paper for Printed Library
Materials, ANSI/NISO Z39.48–1992.

For

GREG DENING

History's anthropologist

STANLEY DIAMOND

Anthropology's poet

CONTENTS

IV. SHADES OF SCIENCE

V. SELF AND OTHER

VI. SEMIOTICA

Illustrations

ACKNOWLEDGMENTS

Long ago I settled into the idea that poetry has to be more than gushing over sunsets. But I have not abandoned such practices altogether and consider myself most fortunate to be in a position to do some genuine gushing here. The debts I incurred moving through the tides and ports of this project are many and large. What appears here has benefitted piecemeal or in the overall from generous commentary by Laurel Richardson, Barbara Tedlock, Mac Marshall, Jon Sisk, Judy McCulloh, Margery Wolf, Don Mitchell, Thomas F. Powell, Charles D. Laughlin, Jr., Edie Turner, Iain Prattis, Alok Kumar, DeWight Middleton, Dan Ingersoll, Norman Weiner, Laura Wrubel, Paul Benson, Donna Merwick, Edward O'Shea, Erin Fiorini, Tom Loe, Stephen Saraydar, John W. Presley, Scott Gardner, John Ross, Mary Becker, Jr., Lewis Turco, Kathleen Brady Ortega, Jeanne Simonelli, Robert Borofsky, George Marcus, Shiela Murphy, and three departed friends, Stanley Diamond, Toni Flores, and Henry Lundsgaarde, who were instrumental in reviving my commitment to write poetry. I am also grateful to Lola Romanucci-Ross, hands-down the best epistolary friend on the planet, who urged me to get on with the task at hand and then, with superior patience and insight, helped me read it in every incarnation; artist, poet, anthropologist Dan Rose for sharing his immense creative gifts and careful attention; Angela Galvin, Annette Valentine, Linda Lagoe, Sandy Emeterio, and Jim Ford for assistance with production; poet Tracy Lewis for his inspiring translation of this book into Spanish; Sara Varhus for enlightening conversations and enthusiasm for this project; poet and anthropologist Miles Richardson for his cogent and persistent explorations of humanistic writing and for making his critical eye available on demand; Mitch Allen for trusting me and for bringing everything together at AltaMira; Norman K. Denzin and Yvonna Lincoln for extensive readings, wise counsel, steadfast encouragement, and countless other forms of essential help; Michael Salpeter, stalwart friend and eternal spark, for knowing what is important and how to get to it; linguist and anthropologist Dell Hymes for learned advice and for pioneering so much that matters to so many in anthropological poetics; Greg Dening for his poetic prose, profound sense of history, fascination with the sea, and two well-tested decades of friendship; and, not least, James A. Boon for the same decades of camaraderie and the best possible instructions on how to love words. Thinking about thanking also reminds me that I am rich with love in word and deed from my family, Todd, Tye, Christa, Bridget, Sophia, and my wife and fellow traveler Jane. All of the art in this book is in one way or another hers: in her treasured paintings, of course, which she has graciously shared with us, but also in the shape of the thoughts and words her work has pulled from me on this and so many other occasions. These wonderful people are my wind, sail, and structure. I thank them all.

Permissions

"Predator" first appeared in *Anthropology and Humanism Quarterly* 9 (4), 1984, p. 25; "Pueblo Canyon" in *Reflections: The Anthropological Muse,* edited by Ian Prattis, Washington, D.C.: American Anthropological Association, 1985, pp. 86-94; "Cannibal-*ism*" in *Anthropology and Humanism Quarterly* 11 (4), 1986, p. 87; "Killing Death" in *Anthropology and Humanism* 23 (1), 1998, pp. 3-4. They are reprinted with permission of the American Anthropological Association. "Memory Sweep" was originally published in the *Neuroanthropology Network Newsletter* 2 (1), 1989, p. 2; "My Friend Henry" is adapted from my obituary for Henry Peder Lundsgaarde in the *Association for Social Anthropology in Oceania Newsletter* 103, April, 1999, pp. 24-5. Several pieces appeared in *Qualitative Inquiry (QI):* "A Gift of the Journey" was published in *QI* 4 (4), 1998, p. 463; "The Visitor" appeared with another poem, "Kultur House," in *QI* 5 (4), 1999, pp. 566-7; "Jaguar," "Spot of the Cat," and "Archaeology?" were published as "Three Jaguar/Mayan Intertexts: Poetry and Prose Fiction" in *QI* 6 (1), 2000, pp. 58-62; "The Equation" appeared in *QI* 6 (3) 2000, pp. 435-7; "Border Work," "The Shape of Time," and "Fieldwork Pastiche" were published in *QI* 7 (6), 2001, pp. 808-10; "Show Me a Sign," "Torn Shawl," and "Pipers" were published in *QI* 8 (2), 2002, pp. 175-9—a special issue on the 9/11/01 tragedies in America; "Proem for the Queen of Spain" was published in *Cultural Studies ⇔Critical Methodologies* 1 (4), 2001, pp. 517-9. They are reprinted with permission from Sage. "Fire Knees," "Festival," "Island Chains," and "When You Were Here" appeared in *drunken boat: online journal of the arts*, 3, fall/winter, 2001-2002. They are reproduced with permission from drunkenboat.com.

"Trying to find the other by defining otherness or by explaining the other through laws and generalities is, as Zen says, like beating the moon with a pole or scratching an itching foot from the outside of a shoe."

—Trinh T. Minh-ha, *Woman, Native, Other*

"…it is the narrative that is the life of the dream while the events themselves are often interchangeable. The events of the waking world on the other hand are forced upon us and the narrative is the unguessed axis along which they must be strung. It falls to us to weigh and sort and order these events. It is we who assemble them into the story which is us. Each man is the bard of his own existence. This is how he is joined to the world."

—Cormac McCarthy, *Cities of the Plain*

"Talk is never bare words, of course. It is all the ways words are symbolised. It is voice and gesture, rhythm and timing, colour and texture. Talk is tattoo. Talk is body paint and house columns. Talk is never just stream of consciousness either. It is shaped and dramatised —in a dance, a song, a story, a joke. Talk is silence. Talk might seem to be blown away by the wind on the lips, but it never is. It is always archived in some way in the continuities of living."

—Greg Dening, Address to the Pacific History Association, Canberra, June 28, 2000

"I want you to feel what I felt. I want you to know why story-truth is truer sometimes than happening-truth."

—Tim O'Brien, *The Things They Carried*

INTRODUCTION

There is something inherently anthropological and poetic about the process of twisting the familiar into strange and showing the strange to be familiar. Through instructions on how to look and how to find, a poet might be able to enhance or derail for wider purposes the text of any experience, depending on what is revealed versus what is expected by the reader. As students of the extraordinary, and perhaps of finding it in unexpected— including ordinary—places, the anthropologist joins the poet in hoping that such manipulations reveal much and wreck nothing beyond complacency about the nature of the world and our place in it. In that connection, I present *The Time at Darwin's Reef* primarily as a book of storytelling through mixed genres— verse, prose, and painting. It should be enjoyed in that capacity. However, on the premise that the same text can do other work as well, my intention is also to draw out some key dimensions of the poetics of anthropology and history embedded in creative writing—in the mix and on the margins of verse and prose, painting and writing, fiction and fact—to revisit the sometimes academically resistant idea that there is more than one way to say (and therefore to see) things. This is a poetic exploration of many themes encountered in the academic world's attempts to explicate reality, including travel through various cultures, times, and circumstances. The poetic commitment makes it at once less an effort "to get the name and address of every event in the universe," as Kenneth Burke once said of logical positivism, and more an effort to move in the same direction on vastly different terms, to engage all manner of experience through the more encompassing realm of what Burke understood so well to be poetic meaning.[1] As a tiny slice of that larger agenda, I offer here poetics with a footprint, a fingerprint, and a calendar—a diary of sorts, a torn travel ticket left on the bar by an earlier patron, a

---

[1] Kenneth Burke, "Semantic and Poetic Meaning," IN *The Philosophy of Poetic Form,* Berkeley: University of California Press, 1973, pp. 136-67.

clue, a glimpse, a trace of having been and of moving on, a bare scattering of marks on a slate of enormous possibilities. History and anthropology are made of such things.

The goal of this little book is thus both aesthetic and analytic. It is also humanistic: commentary on the human condition through a slim history of looking and finding, being and not being, in a cross-cultural world. That may appear to be a big burden to carry in so small a package, but it really isn't. Most texts can be read at several different levels and most of what matters here—meaning evoked in the reader—is only weighty in other ways. Adding something as simple as datelines to this work, for example, is designed to stretch that evocation and to support the mining of both aesthetic and analytic interests. More than just another semiotic marker or poetic line, the datelines ultimately link up with more complicated things, including issues of authenticity and validity, textual authority and voice, not to mention mimesis and the various forms of authorial representation in texts. Their most immediate function is to create or enhance a twofold concern for time and place in each piece. Our ability to construct time and place from such laconic texts, Miles Richardson asserts with insight, is "one of the unsung contributions of our interpretive capacity, our facility to give narrative coherence, and thus meaning, to the many signs that inhabit the text of our lives. Given the sketchiest sentence or the most fragmented action, we fill in the gaps to produce a lucid account of what we, you and I, are up to."[2] We are compelled to interpret such signs and cues about our environment because, in a general sense, our very existence as human creatures depends on it. Our deeply evolved sense of place is strong, tied among other things to natality, kinship, and mortality; to sacred and personal space, spiritual help, travel, the seasons, and the calendar. Personal space is a collecting center for experience and

---

[2] Miles Richardson, "Place, Narrative, and the Writing Self: The Poetics of Being in *The Garden of Eden," The Southern Review,* 35 (2), Spring 1999, p. 334; for more on this process, illustrated in frustration, see Italo Calvino's metafiction, *If On A Winter's Night A Traveler*, New York: Knopf, 1981.

identity construction and a center for *re*collection that can be variously hoarded and shared with others. When that is tapped by text or tale, we are implicated in the story by the process.

The general effect of reading this writing in the context of the datelines is plainly a poetic and a rhetorical function which compels us to read the work differently. So powerful is this cuing, this cultural and psychological bent for sorting time and place, that even the appended lists of the dates and places coded in this work can function as feeding grounds for our imaginary locators, a feast for swift travelers of mind—and a fountain for new questions. Is place really the anchor of all such experiences? Do we recognize it? Know enough about it to enjoy a fanciful imagining of passage there? If you visit a place at three separate times, is it still the same place? Does the place remember you? The answers are as much a function of landscape evolving as they are of finders finding what they want or need to see—a cultural meaning and orientation problem with historical implications. We are compelled to read beyond the proprietary claims of the author's name into something more specifically historical, the biographical. Was the author there? Is this part of the author's identity? Having hooked that in the author's text, empathy for the situation prompts an autobiographical sense of history and identity in comparison: Have I been there? Is this me? Mine? Can I imagine it? Do I understand it? Do I care?

How the answers are both elicited and given matters. Empathy should reign in creative communication. Written or spoken, specifiable history or not, the best of it should stir up something personal and caring in the consumer, even as it draws on the same properties in its own authorial emergings, in the formation of its own possibilities for meaningful connections to the times, geographies, cultures, desires, and imaginations of others—ultimately yielding a specific context of interpretation. Poetic reading makes that specificity generalizable as aesthetic context. Data masters will chase the details. The most pleasurable texts will find some common ground between the two. That's why some texts in anthropology and history look suspiciously like literature. Here, it is enough to get a sense of the cultural and historical framework as part of the overall aesthetic experience. Specifying time and place both facilitates and constrains that in special ways.

Despite the emphasis on time and place as components of conveyable history, there are few obvious sequences from piece to piece and there is no overall chronological order to this work. To raise consciousness (and criticism) of the constructions and boundaries that implicitly define anthropological and historical writing—knowledge production in those fields—I have created what George Marcus has called a "messy text."[3] It does several pedagogic and aesthetic jobs simultaneously and few of them exactly according to established disciplinary interests or form. Culturally, much of this work clusters around the Pacific Islands and México, but it is single-minded or conventional anthropology and history only in the breach of what is normally expected in the academic setting of detached observers. Flagged by its poeticity,[4] this material is written to be read as much more personally and reflexively engaged with the subject matter (e.g., in terms of how the book as a whole fits into *my* personal history as an anthropologist, *my* sense of personal engagement with these cultures *in relation to* yours, the history of *my* own writing in relation to the history of *your* reading it, etc.). Similarly, comparisons amongst the individual datelines can be instructive, and some are explicitly intended to be read that way. But the first function of the datelines is to contextualize each individual piece for time and place. The dates I have assigned add an important dimension to the intellectual and aesthetic possibilities of the text. As particular statements, however, they are all significant to

---

[3] George Marcus, "What Comes (Just) After 'Post'? The Case of Ethnography." IN *Handbook of Qualitative Research,"* edited by Norman K. Denzin and Yvonna S. Lincoln. Thousand Oaks, CA: Sage, 1994, pp. 563-74. See also Norman K. Denzin, *Interpretive Ethnography: Ethnographic Practices for the 21ˢᵗ Century*, Thousand Oaks, CA: Sage, 1997.
[4] See Ivan Brady, "Anthropological Poetics." IN *Handbook of Qualitative Research*, edited by Norman K. Denzin and Yvonna S. Lincoln, 2ⁿᵈ ed., Thousand Oaks, CA: Sage, 2000, pp. 949-79.

me but would seem to be truly potluck in their possible connections to readers. Still, whether or not the particular day or month named counts for anything (perhaps suggesting holidays, seasons), some readers will "get" the overall set and read in a rich context because of their own histories. Some will just get a sense of the moment and move on to the words that follow. Some won't care and will scan on with a tidbit of meaning filed away. There is no fixed or "correct" level of aesthetic consumption, only different forms and levels of interpretation and satisfaction. But, this time keeping with conventional interests in history, the generalizable combination of time *and* place seems to be the key to the most evocative readings, aesthetic or otherwise.[5] It is not just Paris, but French culture *in* Paris 1929—when the Left Bank was thriving with philosophers and the world was still proving possible what we thought were its impossibilities, including failure of the American stock market that year, and so forth.

For the aesthetic traveler, the non-archaeologist, the historian on holiday, the datelines can be passed through without much contemplation, moving in even flow on to the writings they cap. That does not wreck the text. It may be the best path for the poetic experiences intended. Being analytic about aesthetics under the same cover, however, *is* playing with fire and can certainly wreck the aesthetic experience. It is possible to destroy a poetic reading completely by analyzing it to death. So some caution is required to avoid defeating the primary purpose in this multi-purpose book, which is both to inform *and* entertain and to

---

[5] The universality of the categories (not the cultural particulars) of time and space makes it difficult to separate the paths of their conjunctions. One could argue that place is probably the primary factor in dateline equations, if for no other reason than the fact there is considerable poetic power in specifying or implying place without specifying time, while the reverse seldom makes any sense at all, at least in the mechanics of composition. Cf. Robert Levine on Judaism: "The prophets teach that the day of the Lord is more sacred than the house of the Lord. Temporal settings, rather than spatial ones, frame the sacred Jewish texts" (*A Geography of Time,* New York: Basic Books, 1997, p. 208).

do so largely by writing in the realm of the possible, not necessarily the actual.

Determining what is true versus what "rings true" versus what cannot be true in poetic writing also makes a difference of interpretation. Slipping into this web, we ask: Are the circumstances of each piece real (the author was actually there at that time)? Or fictional (the author was there only by inference, imagination being the only transport; temporality invented by the author, no such activity in our physical reality at that time)? Are the places actual locations (existing in the boss reality as occupied space, or once occupied space, and can be rediscovered by going there in person, touching the landscape, and meeting people, or meeting whatever is met by archaeology)?[6] Let me answer by saying that I have taken advantage of the human capacity for artifice and embellished everything in one way or another. I have deliberately blurred genres and therefore mixed up a lot of things, including conventional reporting of the Truth, as a way of marking the boundaries or, in some cases, calling attention to their inherent fuzziness. Some of this work is verse. Knowing full well that poetry can be cast as prose or verse and that the boundary between them is therefore ambiguous at that level, some of what I have included here nonetheless is writing perhaps best described as prose (or description minus obvious or overriding tropes) in verse clothing. Poetic line phrasing flags the writing as "poetic" but does not necessarily make a poem. It gives one sign of a poem but does not necessarily transform the work into poetry in any particularly satisfying or conventional measure. That is a function of deeper structural work in metering or rhythm and form (but not necessarily rhyme) and the semiotics shared in writer/reader relations—of language somehow elevated to higher functions. By the same token, some of this writing is prose best described as poetry (precisely because of its tropes). Some of it is verse set against

---

[6] For an exquisite rendering that blurs the boundaries of all of these strategic dimensions in a single text, see Dennis Tedlock's *Days from a Dream Almanac*, Urbana: University of Illinois Press, 1990.

conventional prose as a way of developing different story contexts and aspects of a common topic (jaguars, for example, as implied in "Predator" and its relationship to the trilogy of "Jaguar," "Spot of the Cat," and "Archaeology?").

It follows that some of the poetic circumstances in this book are authentic and valid, some are stretched to fit the context I was trying to produce in the piece, and some are obviously fictions in the conventional sense of that term. Limiting themselves to the habits of thought and established genres of their objectivities and therefore asking only the wrong questions for the purposes of this book, fact masters may want to know precisely which is which and they will be frustrated by the fictions. I make no apologies for that. The mix is a way to remind ourselves of the difficulties of ideological discernment and cultural calculation, of writing and representation, especially in cross-cultural settings. It is a way to re-explore the shadowed but continuous ground that seems to cleave erroneously into hard fences for disciplines, separating the fictional from the factual. Through some conspiracy of not crossing the field of our collective writings in the light of day, we do not (or do not want to) see that the fence is made of old straw. Fiction can be closer to life than some fact masters will allow, and practically everything can be represented both ways. In the wake of postmodern challenges to author-*ity* on these issues, I have taken both the daylight and the larger field of our writings seriously and tried to turn the sometimes frustrating process of winnowing truth from the chaff of experience back upon itself. I've tried to put it back in the chaff as poetic artifice and hope that it will not be disguised or reduced in the process—that it will be discoverable and re-discoverable as enriched knowledge through the commonalities and creativities of our experience as readers and writers. But even that has a curious link with our senses of time and place and the study of history and anthropology.

All writing is fictional, as Clifford Geertz once said about anthropology (and Hayden White about history), in the sense of being something constructed, something made through interpretation, and never out of whole cloth. It is a mix of constraints, easily exaggerated by special interests. Working both sides to make the point, we can say that nothing comes purely from the imagination, on the one hand, and the degree to which any work is grounded in empirical reality, as it is usually argued, is easily overestimated, on the other. Like other domains in the academy (and life in general), anthropology and history follow suit. They are burdened with cultural and imaginative impositions in their attempts to be factual, to portray the world accurately as it "is" or presents itself to the observer who would be objective. Conversely, the novelist can take the same principle and pass over actuality in facts and behavior, arguing perhaps for a string of events never seen or heard before. But plausibility and the fundamentals of communication assure some grounding in empirical reality. The work would otherwise fail. The larger point is that interpretation is as necessary to life as breathing. The interpretive quotient can be constrained through language and method, but it cannot be avoided. The capacity to represent the world in any manner we desire is fundamental to culture. We can lie or tell the truth according to a variety of standards, most of which are culturally specific. The power of the imagination inherent in that makes us both good novelists and scientists, that is to say, creators and calculators of substance and time, pasts, presents, and futures. We are anthropological and historical narrators, storytellers all.

As an arbitrary slice of the universal categories of time and location, history in the particular (*of* something, *as* a partial narrative whose beginning and ending points are determined by the teller) is shot through with such constraints. On the continuum of time that can be read forward and backward, the common view is that making history is a one-way street. It looks back in time and compares that necessarily with interpretations of the present, but back is the focus nonetheless. Nothing is history until it has happened in the here and now, and it can't be "true" in any sense until it has a chance to pass us in time, going backwards. By contrast, going the other direction, what might be called "future history" is fiction in every sense of the term. The future context in which I contemplate my own death in the "Dead Painting" poem (Ireland 2023), for example, takes away the conventional historical dimension—for now. The fact that I have already written it makes the writing event itself a kind of history, but not the argument of the text. That's a separate reality, a speculation, plainly a fiction, and out of historical time. "Probable" is probably the best truth hedge for the future. Science fiction is the extreme hedge, hard to assess as probable, and definitely not history. It can be poetry or a part of poetry, however, and does figure into the equation of "Para Donde Vas" —a narrative poem that has implied time in real places. It is a story that holds a promise of conventionally factual history, but the promise is not fulfilled. The expectation of ordinary reality is broken through poetic license, that is, by manipulating literary form and premise for creative ends.

Reversing directions again, to the extreme past as opposed to the speculative future, I've tried to do similar things with myth. Classic (or autochthonous) myth is to be discovered, read, internalized, translated, repeated, or in other ways explicated. It can be told in whole or in part and re-telling is always a kind of rewriting, a creative act by definition.[7] But rewriting fundamentals of structure or message can change the category (e.g., to parody or other forms of narrative), so there are limits. The Western cultural bias against myth as something necessarily false only confuses the issue: not recognizing the inescapability of mythic structures in the first place, and holding the idea of

---

[7] I refer here to the general cognitive process of creative mimesis. It is inherent in all forms of representation and translation, intentional or not. Overt recognition of its transformational properties is probably as old as orature itself and it shows up as a topic in various philosophical and literary discourses. Bertolt Brecht made much of it in his work on originality in theater. It is also institutionalized as storyteller functions in the Brazilian *Literatura de Cordel* (see Candace Slater, *Stories on a String*, Berkeley: University of California Press, 1982) and Méxican *corridos* (see Américo Paredes, *Folklore and Culture on the Texas-Mexican Border*, Austin: University of Texas Press, 1995).

new adapatations of older structures aside, nobody wants a "new" myth. The very concept is seen at best as an oxymoronic amusement and at worst as fakery. Even where the long run continuity of mythic writing with the defining narratives of our times is better understood and respected, recent writing posed as myth is still likely to be assigned to a special category of fiction or interpretation that only emulates more ancient histories and therefore depends on a prior or perhaps more highly generalized and cross-cultural version to enter the debate concerning historical accuracy and related truth claims (Mormons have taken this one on the chin for a long time). I've called to mind for possible criticism the knottiness of these issues most directly in "The Spring," "Fire Knees," "Gilbertese Warrior," and "Spot of the Cat"—each of which has a legitimate claim to authenticity but is nonetheless nested in the wax of my creativity—and again through the mix of history with mythic implications in the more imaginative framing and less authentic storylines of "Shipwreck" and "Para Donde Vas." A fair reading of these pieces can defend the argument that mythic writing doesn't have to be authentically or overtly ancient in text or context to be recognized and celebrated as such or to carry legitimate claims to the truth of action reported and social or moral lessons inferred. And it hardly needs to be said, as in the case of future oriented fiction or biblical precedents, that mythic writing can be poetry or a part of poetry and more—classic poetics. It is for the most part simply a matter of form and expectations.

 In narratives about the past or present as well as expectations about the future, irrespective of discipline or cultural orientation, the truth is necessarily relative to what is seen as possible, rational, and desirable in the reality framework the observers use (and may prefer to any others)—a possible disparity illustrated by the competing perspectives in my ethnographically authentic long poem, "Pueblo Canyon," and the laconic pairing of "Midnight Swim" with "Letter from Laurie." Like life itself, war happens from different perspectives and everybody knows something about the range of variations and storied outcomes.

The soldier's view is not necessarily that of the sweetheart and, despite their linkages in time and space, their stories may never match. Each is in important ways necessarily "outsider" to the other. But juxtaposing these differences starkly should evoke a larger text in the reader, a creative reading and launching into larger realms, a closure of sorts anchored in the reader's personal beliefs, desires, and experiences, that is, in the cultural preparation the reader brings to the event regarding its personal and cultural implications. The wedding of writing to painting should also create a new text between the texts of the paintings and the words on the page. Not only can we construct time and place with amazing lucidity and realism from laconic cues; we can build whole narratives from mixed packages of them with equal facility. I've tried to exploit that prospect by presenting diverse texts that make some links obvious and some informational gaps conspicuous among written texts and between written texts and paintings, and that puts a special emphasis on comparative differences within and between works —anthropology's first principle.[8]

Nothing stands alone in language and no single form or genre can say it all. If anything, the present texts move in the other direction. They are intentionally plural and incomplete. On careful inspection, they should suggest more than they say, and

---

[8] The original paintings are signed and dated in their interiors and in that sense display their own "histories." But (unlike the copyrights) that information is not equally visible on the plates as represented here. The signatures and dates have slipped largely from history to mystery as an artifact of the reproduction process for this book. Moreover, while the paintings imply specific locations by "showing" place, neither they nor their titles resolve the ambiguities of exactly where. Such lacunae further exemplify the unfightable thesis that ethnographic and biographical information is by definition incomplete, always laconic at some level, always inviting new readings, new interpretations, and new satisfactions, personal and otherwise, only in this case through very different forms. Overall, the paintings punctuate the external text without ever duplicating it exactly, at one level, while simultaneously opening up new paths of interpretation and exploration, at another, thereby adding yet another voice (and conception of beauty) to the author's as each unveils geographies of fieldwork in strange places.

like other relations between makers and mindful others in the world of print and paint, they should link up in a joint project. Continuity of theme and thesis can only transcend such gaps through the creative cooperation of presenter (writer, painter) and consumer (reader, viewer). I have steered toward my own preferred interpretations and conclusions in what I have said and the manner of its placement relative to other parts of the book, of course, but I have not made many of these connections explicit beyond the tropes and arguments of each individual piece. Storytellers and readers in search of larger contexts, emotional reinforcement of their own passions and prejudices about being in the world, and so on, will fill the gaps with their own material. Texts are made and remade with every exposure. They are not necessarily remade radically and there may be great consistency of message and meaning between a particular writer and readers. Successful communication and social coherence depend on that kind of prospect. But every individual reading is nonetheless a personal remake and therefore a candidate for reinvention at new and hitherto undiscovered levels of comprehension, criticism, and satisfaction. That's the way the system works, no matter what penchants the reader brings to the project.

It takes no genius to conclude that there are larger thoughts and patterns of interpretation and levels of satisfaction to be had in the present work. I have offered no overriding analytic thesis beyond these few introductory comments on the nature of writing and reading in shadowed territory, and what is conventional in this writing can justify an equally conventional reception. But this is also writing laced with a twist or two on differences in life and culture and the various forms we use to represent our experiences with them. It raises some uncommon flags in the alleys and backwashes of genres and forms that academics in particular have come to depend on for predictable (or less troublesome) readings, if not for scholarly dissertations on the nature of the world and our place in it. The writing in this book represents other ways to talk about the same things. The focus on time and place and story-making fits these larger interests and, more particularly, the variable frames and forms of experience attached to Darwin's Reef—the book, the poem, the experience of being there, the scoring of comparable experiences for different readers, different divers in different moments, my time, your time. Where you go with it depends largely on where you start, what you seek or perhaps need to find. Anthropology and history are all over this book but you may have to work to find them in some cases. A closer look may let you find them on several levels at once. The anthropology and history of the Reef poem, for example, are staked in part by the dateline, coded in my account of the ecology of the place, in the social relations entailed by and revealed about the events reported, in the self-revelations and other snippets of autobiographical identity contained in the text, and in the act of writing about these things, the cultural and cognitive processes of production itself. They are further constituted in important ways by what we (you and I) make of this work in the staggered time frames and largely open loop relationships of author and reader—some of which may be closed by reviews and other forms of feedback. There is also a history or two to be had in the review process, of course, and the culture of it all—representing the world through research, writing, reading, reviewing, and maybe even press parties—is fair game for any ethnographer. That is part of what makes The Reef such a rich place. It is a state of mind and more, and you can get there from here. Spill some thought on these pages and rehydrate the traveling. I've put notes as guideposts on some of it and left other parts alone. Make what you will of each piece and the overall, aesthetically and analytically, remembering that context is practically everything for determining meaning. My sincerest wish is that you will find pleasure in the journey.

IB, Fountain Hills, Arizona, June 9, 2002

I. GATEWAY

Cattermaller Swamp, Louisiana,
April 13, 1941

ALONE ON
THE BAYOU

ankle-deep in
brackenwash

lucky
for the
moment
to be no one
in particular

mostly silent
unreflected

Gulf of California
July 14, 1952

SEA CREAM

foggy dreams
airbrushed on green
floating low
across the beam
dissipate
in gulps of steam

PLATE 1. *Escultura Coral.* Watercolor
by Janie Brady, ©1999.

Puerto Rico,
January 14, 1998

DIVING IN
DESECHEO

I saw
the sea
and the
sea saw
me. We
agreed
to meet
again.

Soon.

II. MYTHICS

6

THEY KNEW PLACES WHERE

A man could crawl up in a wormhole
    No bigger than his head
Vampires served as lifeguards
    And pools were full of blood

Sea life lived forever
    But evening skies could die
Birds took over cities
    And all the cars could fly

Falling was only backwards
    And nothing hit the ground
Music came from eggshells
    And was laid upon the land

Days were always longest
    When night ran out of time
Poets wrote the books
    But could not read a line

Prizes went to losers
    And armies always won
Sins of a wayward father
    Could not ignite the son

Lovers courted seedlings
    And sex came from a gourd
A man could crawl inside a woman
    And always be reborn

Fa'apoto Island, March 21, 1799

FALE TAPU

No man was allowed to eat from a woman's plate
Or to touch her person or her belongings when she bled
Or to eat the food she prepared when she bled
Or to see her private parts at such times of the cycle
Or to talk rudely of her condition when the tide pulls

No man was allowed to set his head higher than a chief
Or to touch the hair or person or belongings of a chief
Or to see a chief's private parts when he sat or urinated
Or to eat the food prepared for a chief or discarded by him
Or to talk rudely of his condition when the tide pulls

No man was allowed to say the name of the god in public
Or to say the name of the name of the god while hungry
Or to say the name of the name of the god while fishing
Or to say the name of the name of the god while angry
Or to talk rudely of the god's condition when the tide pulls

No man was allowed to sacrifice animals when his wife bled
Or to set them in holy places if a chief had cut his hair there
Or to step in chiefly footprints leading to sacrificial ground
Or to whisper the name of the name of the god in sacrifice
Or to talk rudely of sacrificial conditions when the tide pulls

No man was allowed to resist banishment by an island chief
Or to punish himself in public if a chief had urinated there
Or to give his family to sacrifice in caves or cliffs of the sea
Or to say the name of the god when banished to the open sea
Or to talk rudely of the island's condition when the tide pulls

Fa'apoto Island, March 21, 1899

THE SPRING

Rediscovery of the spring erased constraints, including the island taboos and new impositions from the colonials. Identities washed away. Bodies were reduced to nude and meaningless display. They lost the ability to be naked. Food was consumed without preference or joy. Relatives died and were walked over. No one had cloth. No one cared about colors. Perfume was wasted on the air. Houses had shapes but did not cluster. Roads went somewhere but no one could say for sure which direction, and no one cared. Children and adults used the weapons of hand and mind with impunity. The culture of fear was erased. So was the culture of grouping. Signs of belonging vanished in the white blood of the spring, diluted to neutral in the place of all crossings and no crossings, the juncture of the invisible, where all significance is lost to discerning eyes and the senses. It was the well of true beginning: before knowledge, before meaning. It created change even as it cured it. Island culture could only resurrect itself with a mixture of that water, ancient beliefs, and old rules for social behavior, with that and beliefs about the invalidity of beliefs and rules for breaking rules—with criticism and constraint. Only then could the water of true nothingness be reconverted to the original colors, a heartfelt handshake and embrace, a birthing celebration, a dying regret, a social fabric that raveled to all without breaking and made them complete in their parts, separate but joined. So they drank from the spring and spoke sparingly of the original ways. Some spoke more than others, some not at all. When the steam and the murmuring cleared, some of the people were whole again, some were not. The children put down their arms. The groups marked themselves with red dye and blue flowers and made their villages round. Some sailed north to fish. Some stayed home to dance and tell stories of the longest times. They renewed their centers, the spring receded shortly thereafter, and a centrifugal feeling swept all of the intruders out to sea.

"Fire Knees" *is a composite of a story told to me several times during my fieldwork on the atolls and reef islands of Tuvalu (Ellice Islands) in the late 1960's and early 1970's. The context of this story is the founding of the islands, which by all indications would seem to be about four or five hundred years ago as people arrived in odd lots from other islands, mostly with ties to Samoa, and like most origin myths, it has a didactic tilt— lessons for the moment from moments long ago. Fish and probably the ubiquitous coconut palm were the primary resources available for human subsistence at the time. Taro, pulaka root, and pigs were imported. Coconut trees have been imported and planted by migrants in various parts of the Pacific. But the floating nut has voyage patterns of its own. Cannibalism also figures as a common theme in accounts (apochryphal or otherwise) of early ocean voyaging and settlement. The prospect of eating another human is always present in social groups, of course, however deeply proscribed, and it gets more conscious attention everywhere under periods of prolonged distress or deprivation. But its actual practice is also commonly exaggerated and misunderstood, especially by Westerners who have swallowed their own colonial mentalities whole and have a penchant for racist or related superiority stances against the Others of the world. The myth suggests that* Tulivaepula (tulivae = knee; pula = bright or glowing) *was both big enough to have a large appetite and to enforce it, even if it meant eating other people. It also contains a thesis on cooked versus raw food and gives instructions on the social and survival value (happiness, harmony, productivity) of a more diverse diet that includes indigenous and imported foods and bypasses the violence and destructiveness of cannibalism. By the way, the dateline in this poem opens another voice beyond mine. It implies that the story was told by someone else at a particular moment a long time ago. That builds on the often nebulous and pseudo-historical implications of all myth and brings the content into history per se, in this case, the history of the telling of a myth. Whether or not the story and the history of its telling are true as presented is another problem.*

Funafuti Island, Tuvalu, October 12, 1492

FIRE KNEES (OR, NOT EATING RAOUL)

Samumuta and Samumutai were friends. One night they went fishing with hand nets on the reef. They could not fail. Mesmerized by the blazing torch fixed on the canoe prow, fish were everywhere. They streamed to the nets and were lifted, pound after pound, into the canoe. "Tapa!" the friends exclaimed with every haul. "Tapa! Tapa! What a catch!"

Then the rain came and put out the torch.

Samumuta and Samumutai tried to relight the torch but it was too wet. Fumbling and grumbling in the darkness, they scanned the horizon and spotted a fire burning on a far shore. "Aha!" they thought. "We can relight our torch with that fire." They paddled into the current, raised the sail, and steered to the distant islet, eating raw fish on the way.

The breakers pushed the canoe ashore. The two young men got out and raced toward the fire. It had a curious glow. Each time they held their torch to it, the torch would not burn. Puzzled, they poked at the fire with their fingers and discovered that it was not a fire at all. It was someone's knee! A knee scarred bright red that was attached to a giant leg attached to a giant man, a man-eating ogre named Tulivaepula, who was kneeling on the beach. "Here is something for me to eat!" he boomed. "You two shall be my food!"

"Please do not eat us," said the two young men. "We can work for you. You can see from our canoe full of fish that we are quite capable." But the ogre resisted. He said that he was able to do his own work and reached down to snatch the two men and eat them. "Wait! Please wait!" they shouted. "Give us a chance to prove ourselves!" Thinking he could eat them and their fish whenever he chose, the ogre finally relented. Besides, he had sore knees from reaching out into the ocean for his own fish and he could use some rest. "Very well," he said, "but you must fish for me every day."

The three of them lived together for a long time. Samumuta and Samumutai did not return home. They caught fish for themselves and the ogre under the ogre's watchful eye. Then one day no fish appeared. No fish could be caught. The two men asked the ogre to let them go to an islet across the lagoon to continue fishing for all of them. The ogre resisted, thinking this was just a ruse to escape to their homes. He reached down to them and said, "No. You cannot go. Come along with me and prepare the oven."

When that was done the scarred-knee ogre made a new demand. He told the youths to wrestle and declared that the loser would be cooked in the oven for the day's food. They wrestled hard, fearing Tulivaepula's immediate wrath for both of them, and Samumuta was thrown to the ground.

Samumutai hauled his friend to the oven and put him inside. After a while Tulivaepula told Samumutai to open the oven. The food should be cooked. He opened the oven and there was Samumuta alive! He was not and could not be cooked! Thankful for his good fortune, Samumuta leapt from the oven only to reveal another surprise. In his place were many different kinds of food: taro, pulaka root, pork, and fish. The ogre and the two men gathered these foods and feasted happily together from that day forward.

"Gilbertese Warrior" *draws closely on my Pacific Islands fieldwork and on a reading of Ernest Sabatier's classic,* Astride the Equator: An Account of the Gilbert Islands *(Melbourne: Oxford University Press, 1977, pp. 125ff.). See also Arthur Grimble's* "Myths from the Gilbert Islands" (Folk-Lore *33, pp. 91-112; 34, pp. 370-4, 1922-23).*

Abaiang Island, February 14, 1840

GILBERTESE WARRIOR

When you were twelve
And Antares rose after sunset
You were told to face the fire upwind to the east
Not to move or flinch or look away

Father's father cut your hair with a shark's tooth
Father's brothers made the magic protection
Against weakness and attractions to women
Against fear and cowardice

When you were twenty and two moons
And Antares rose after sunset
You were told to face the fire upwind to the east
Not to move or flinch or look away

Father cut your hair with a shark's tooth all night
Father's brothers beat you with palm fronds
Lit a torch over your head and dripped it on you
And you did not move or flinch or look away

Close to the fire you drank from a coconut shell
Sea water and oil, mixed with a stingray barb
Fumed with incantations, magical strength
While father stabbed his own hair with the tooth

Father's father made your first spear
Seasoned coconut wood twelve feet long
Double rows of shark teeth at the point
Tied on by strands of warrior's hair

Father kept the spear when you were
Sent away to a secluded hut to the east
Where you stayed alone until the roof began to leak
Five years without visitors, without women

Senior men brought you special food, and silence
Grandfather gave you work cutting trees and bushes
Carrying stones, learning tactics, weapons
Shark's tooth swords, sennit armor, war clubs

Learning strength of family, origins, histories
Pushing discipline, the boundaries of hardship
Fathoming grandfather's magic, wisdom
Practicing fighting in the sea, on the reef

Then you were led to the village maneaba
And young men danced in your honor
And young women danced in your honor
And songs were crafted and sung for you

And you were strong, strong they sang
And you were wise, wise they sang
And you were feared, feared they sang
And you were *rorobuaka*—warrior

One day a traitor and a white man from Tarawa
Came to your island and skirted it in a small boat
With a new weapon at hand, a long stick
A cracking noise that killed, a trick of the gods

The warriors formed a ferocious wall on the shore
Tradition and courage in a line, armed and unafraid
The tube smoked with a loud report and nobody understood
It smoked again and a pebble of death pierced your shield

Knocked you down, knocked out your breath
Stole your vision, your strength, your power
Drained your blood, your round pebble magic
Killed your grandfather's pride, your father's son

And the reef turned red that day
And the sky turned silver for a year
And the sea was diseased with iron ships
And the land was swallowed by thunder and smoke

Nanumea Island, Central Pacific, September 6, 1842

WHEN YOU WERE HERE

Morning sun lingered in the lagoon
    Replacing afternoon for three days
        Replacing darkness until midnight
            Replacing the cock's crow at dawn
Coconuts climbed down the trees on the backs of lizards
    And gave themselves to the crabs and me
        And gave themselves to thirsty Tongans
            And gave themselves to the sea at night
Tapa cloth leapt out to sea one playful day
    And made the fish prettier
        And made the dolphins dance upright
            And made the fishermen paddle hard to catch it
Clouds wrapped my head for sleep
    And sailed low on the canoes for twelve days
        And lifted lovers off their sleeping mats at night
            And cast about with fog making islets disappear
Reef came ashore on legs one night
    And cut lumber for a new house
        And asked the men to mend their nets
            And took some crabs home
Sunset came to me in a dress one evening
    And gave me red lips softer than birds
        And showed me orange smoke that soothed the eyes
            And thickened me with desire
Missionary pierced the horizon one day in a ship
    And came ashore in a chair
        And gave himself to the people
            And lifted lovers off their sleeping mats at night
Warrior came ashore one night and took you away
    Slamming my heart with thunder
        Drenching my fire with cloudburst
            Replacing the morning sun with darkness

Northern Slope, Mount Kilimanjaro, November 3, 1999

FOOT QUERIES

Laetoli, Tanzania, 4 million years ago, fresh ash falling...
Two ancient humans, small, upright, walking in sulfur &
steam, concerned about safe passage, press a trail in the ash.
Going where? Carrying what? Names for fire? Each other?

Langebaan Lagoon, South Africa, 117,000 years ago...
Small woman, modern human, curls a big toe in the wet sand
& punctuates the moment forever. Sunny day? Choppy
water? Something else on the horizon? Other humans?

*Fictional Caribbean, 1659...*Robinson Crusoe, shipwrecked
on a quest for slaves, finds his foot smaller than a fresh print
on the beach—threatening his castaway domain, survival,
& escape. Was he ever really alone?

*Real Caribbean, 1719...*Daniel Defoe, himself a castaway
of sorts, living alone, abandoned by his children, financially
ruined, publishes *Robinson Crusoe*—Defoe's footprint on
literature, escape from the island of life. Can we still see him?

*Earth orbit moon, 1969...*Neil Armstrong lands on the moon
& declares, "One small step for man, one giant step for
mankind!" A skeptical Pacific Islander whispers "Hoax, or he
would see the faeries who live there!" Radio lies? Fake prints?

*Trail to the interior, 1999...*Squatting by the campfire,
volcano in the distance, a trail of prints leads to my own
interior. Am I Friday by any other name? Crusoe? South
African? Moon man? One part ancient pair?

Another marking being endowed for the moment in sand.

"Predator," "Jaguar," *and* "Spot of the Cat" *are a trilogy on a common theme, the jaguar.* "Spot" *was inspired by my reading of Anthony Aveni's masterful* Conversing with the Planets: How Science and Myth Invented the Cosmos *(Kodansha: New York, 1992, pp. 77-8), Dennis Tedlock's innovative* Days from a Dream Almanac *(Chicago: University of Illinois Press, 1990), and the rich mythology in Peter G. Roe's* The Cosmic Zygote: Cosmology in the Amazon Basin *(New Brunswick: Rutgers University Press, 1982). I have taken considerable poetic license by imposing the spot interpretation on what had to be in this cultural context an extraordinarily dramatic eclipse of the sun. But little is actually known of the ancient Méxican and Central American jaguar cults or, for that matter, the origin of the Feathered Serpent Quetzalcoatl cult. We do know that the jaguar, while seldom attacking human beings, was the most powerful predator in the Americas, and that the Mayans feared, revered, and emulated it in great detail. The Sun God was believed to take on jaguar characteristics as it passed through the underworld, becoming the tawny jaguar and bound up in that form with fertility and the control of death. The jaguar's unique practice of killing prey by crushing the skull with one snap of its powerful jaws is widely portrayed in ancient art and writing.* "Archaeology" *is historically and thematically linked to* "Spot of the Cat" *and to Chichén Itzá, the place of the great sacrifice following the eclipse in* "Spot," *and therefore to the first two poems in this set as well. Most of my information on Thompson and artifacts discovered in the* cenote *at Chichén Itzá is taken from Charles Gallenkamp's* Maya *(New York: Penguin, 1987, pp. 172-85).*

Mosquito Coast, Lower
Amazon, July 31, 1924

PREDATOR

Seeking
The forest run
The bleeding sun
The edge of breath
A birth in death
    The temple
    By the sea

Smelling
The storage bin
The smoke upwind
The plower's field
A buzzard's meal
    The honied hive
    And the bee

Seeing
The partridge, the hare
The fleeting stare
The beetle's dung
An owl's black tongue
    The ape shape
    In the tree

Hearing
The shuffle, the whine
The shattering vine
The fear in birds
A windless word
    The trapped man
    And the free

Touching
The water, the weed
The senseless deed
The naked brain
A being in pain
     The throbbing
     And the plea

Tasting
The marrow, the stone
The cracking bone
The rush of blood
A soul's dark flood
     The life-lock
     And the key

Finding
The silence, the mirrors
The blush of tears
The pulse of life
Ancestral strife
     The tooth god
     And the litany

Amazon Basin, February 24, 1997

JAGUAR

There, fixed like stone
not five feet away
in the dripping foliage
two black bordered eyes
pumped yellow
by an inner fire
brighter than suns

Ear cups cocked
on a tawny and white face
sculptured intensity
set in the crotch
of a red blossomed tree

Head aimed low
taut shoulders
ringed black spots
barely perceptible
in the scattered shadows
of branches and leaves

Black nostrils flared
over a puff of whiskers
inverted vee mouth
slightly opened
on a white prickly chin

One paw forward
the other nailed
to the tree trunk

He waits

I paralyze, freeze
mesmerized by fierce
and profound beauty

Eye to eye
adrenalin alerts
crossing in staredown
we dance only in the atoms
of our possibilities
and splashing canopy light

No muscle moves

Lightning in my heart
veins pulsing
perspiration
pastes my shirt
cascades down
my neck
backside
puddles in my boots

Stalking?
Surprise encounter?
Palaver?

Emulated and feared
enemy of Anaconda
and Anteater
this is Ocelot Grande
Jaguar God
Day Jaguar
Yellow Jaguar
Sun's Companion
Sky Traveler
Rain Giver
Water Hunter
power animal
to red dye shamans

Male in youth
female in death
quartz crystal semen
Large Ocelot
becomes
Night Jaguar
becomes
Black Moon Jaguar
dangerous panther
cave dweller
animal ruler
of the underworld
water eyes
replace fire
moons replace suns

On this day
the continuum of life
has a chance meeting
of its parts, a silent
tense conversation
spring loaded
with the ripe odors
of anticipation
the closeness of a kill
or a lover, in the ancient
space of anything goes

Life to the swift

Eye movement?

I blink—
the god is gone

Flushed with ecstasy
I catch the Jaguar's perfume
in one sweeping gulp
of the heavy jungle air

Chichén Itzá, Yucatán Peninsula, June 24, 884 A.D.

SPOT OF THE CAT

It is nearly noon and, as predicted by the priests,
The Giant Jaguar spirit has begun to pass in front of the sun.
There for all to see in the waxing ringed spot is the powerful
And terrrifying alliance of Jaguar and Sun God,
Masters of death in the underworld and the overworld,
    Sharing the path of a celestial journey.

At the high edge of the Templo de los Jaguares,
In the midst of carved eagles and jaguars devouring heads,
And the Feathered Serpent and Venus God Quetzalcoatl,
    Five jaguar priests stand alert.

Shadows strike stone columns and the crowd in the courtyard.
Eyes on the priests and the advancing spot on the sun,
    Warriors gather for sacrifice.

First priest, Thirteen Jaguar, speaks to invisible projects
    On this day of great fear.

Spot of the cat takes half the sun and a cool breeze arises.
    Birds alarm in noisy circles overhead.

Serpent Jaguar, second priest, speaks as sky diver Venus,
Lying in hiding, emerges in the darkness,
Brighter in fraternity with the diminishing sun,
    Revealing new wind, new needs.

Jaguar spot takes two thirds of the sun. Third priest,
Jeweled Jaguar, speaks with the wave of a dagger—
    1366 human beings must be sacrificed immediately.

Some are speared as they stand.
Some are dragged to the platform
On top of the most ancient temple.

Backs slammed against the *chacmool* slab,
Black obsidian knives cut beating heart after beating heart,
      And the universal blood runs colder in the retreating
      Sun.

Jaguar spot inches toward the remainder,
      And a flint spark strikes the sky into total darkness.

Fourth priest, Bird Jaguar in mask, speaks to the heavens,
Gestures to the crowd, ten thousand weepers gathered below,
      And the universal blood runs colder in the spot of the
      Cat.

Then, cued by another priestly slash in the air, the Sun God
Renews slowly, Venus disappears, and Giant Jaguar carries
Night in its mouth and slips silently
          Over the green edge of the world
              Into white tousled sea.

Fifth priest, Twenty Jaguarthroats, leads a woeful procession
North to the *cenote* where twenty pregnant women in
Elaborate dresses, jade necklaces and ear plugs, an eight year
Old boy in copper rings, twine apron and a crowning eagle
Mask, stone knives with carved wooden handles, copper bells,
Engraved gold discs, wing-tied parrots, a whistle, incense pots,
Aromatic resin, a dog in coyote skin, clay figurines, turquoise
Toucans, quartz crystals, and countless jars of precious stones
      Are thrown one at a time from a platform
          Into the huge shadowy well.

Bird Jaguar in mask speaks to the heavens and the massive
Crowd below,
      And the colder blood of the universe rivers itself in
      Ritual
          Over the green edge of the world
             Into reddening sea
               And great caverns
                  Of the black ringed
                    Spot of the cat.

Chichén Itzá, Yucatán Peninsula, June 24, 1904

ARCHAEOLOGY?

A large wooden derrick and its dredging apparatus are lined up on the lip of the limestone shelf near the sacrificial platform. After several months of dredging, reclaiming various objects and some skeletal materials, U.S. Consul and Peabody Museum Associate Edward Thompson decides to descend into the pool to explore crevices that the dredge could not reach. His diving equipment consists of an unwieldy dry suit, a heavy helmet with a latched face mask, and a hose connected to a hand driven air compressor above, which is being supervised by two Greek sponge fishermen—and several scores of laborers hired for the project.

Much to the consternation of the Mayan workers, who have a better understanding of the shadows and appetites of the underworld, especially in a place of such great sacred activity, treasure hunter and historical curiositer Thompson descends the ladder and drops off into water that quickly resolves from amber to green and finally to an impenetrable black. Thompson's submarine flashlight is unable to pierce the thick veil of darkness, so he gropes blindly along the floor until he locates a ledge or crevice, then sifts its contents by hand, being careful to avoid the mud wall rocks and tree trunks that, loosened by the relentless dredging, from time to time come plunging down. On this dive Thompson surfaces with a sack full of pottery figurines, an obsidian knife with a carved handle, and the skull of a young boy. He finds artifacts on every dive.

Tossed in hope and awe and wonder in an age whose details were now less accessible than the darkest crevices of the well itself, retrieved as treasure untraceable to the moments of its original meanings, all of the artifacts, like their sacrificers, were silent. They had become shelf pieces, bric-a-brac, storied puzzles for a museum in Massachusetts, where life has no poetry, death no honor, the night sky is blocked by bedroom ceilings, and all of the predators have handguns.

The *cenote* is approximately 200 feet in diameter, 130 feet deep. Its limestone walls rise sixty-five feet above the surface of the murky green water.

From the air, it looks like a ringed spot.

Nantucket Island, Massachusetts
July 4, 1999

YELLOWMOUTH MOON

Eros on parchment, Aphrodite in swoon

Nothing can replace a Yellowmouth Moon

**

With jewels high set, piercing holes in the night

Her darkened blue face exhales lemon light

**

Refracting the sea on a candlelit mirror

Smooth amber lips snail out of her sphere

**

They purse up and fill me with a deep saffron glow

As she makes me her catchman, her golden dipped beau

**

Honeywine sunshine returns in the morn

Lip paint for a New Moon soon to be born

PLATE 2. *Some Moon*. Watercolor by Janie Brady, ©1999.

Ed. Note *4/17/n.s.* *[Archive 3008].* The Joy of Return *is the official publication of the Joy of Return Society* Δ. *Headquartered at Jalapeño Wharf in Venezuela and derived historically from the creative reincarnation and teleportation industries of the popular New Century Yellowmouth Moon Society* Δ, *it specializes in customized reincarnation through a combination of moon-and-self-love and fast travel through an ancient Aztec/Mayan* Δ *gate in the wheel of the sun. It houses the world's largest electronic library of obituaries and offers a free obituary collection and browsing service to families and institutions for a small fee. Special discounts are available for the severely bereaved.*

"Know how to live and you will
know how to die.
Know how to die and you will
know how to live."

—Barancas Paz, Temple Itzpapálotl Δ
Central México 2058.

Museum of Wicca, Salem, Massachusetts, September 23, 2099

TRANSLATED TEXT [Archive 17]

<u>*Notas Técnicas y Alquimias de Lunas*</u>, *Anonymous, Northern Spain, 1077 A.D. Some moons draw more on the tides of seas and people than others. Full moons have such gravity. They are known to drag certain body chemicals into a concentrated pool at the top of the brain that causes the individual to seek new or renew old romantic behavior. People who fail to satisfy this moon induced chemical lust are often given over to vandalism and related unsociable behavior. The same pool creates a lust for blood in lycanthropes, which, if fulfilled, has a calming chemistry of its own. A Yellowmouth Moon is most easily recognized as the quarter moon that shows in the waxing and waning of the full cycle. The lunar face is always shadowed. Discounting the wispy halo that borders the bluish face in these comings and goings, only the mouth glows brightly, and then only in a reclining head smile. No other expression is possible and in that lies a special attribute. The moon's yellow is the fountain of its power and, rather than reducing by three quarters in the one quarter moon, most of the drawing power of a completely lit moon is concentrated in the smile of the more circumspect quarter showing. Poets, songwriters, moon landers [note 1077 A.D. -trans.], and lovers have forever attached their admirations and longings to the full moon, which, although seldom seen as such except by the stone vision people and certain Amazonidan [Amazon] peoples, is in this view a wide open mouth. It can catch you and if can catch you looking, so to speak. It might even kiss you. But the primary point is that the progressive stages of the moon's yellowing are thus measurable and conspicuous changes in*

the openness of the moon's mouth. The body's tide of active dorphinians [endorphins] tends to peak in direct proportion to the lunar yellowness available to it, so a full moon can always be thought of correctly as a "feel good" moon. But because of their concentrated draw, more effort spent absorbing the lumens of circumspect [less than full] moons by gazing at them for equivalent periods of time has an equal prospect for releasing [endorphins] in the body and pooling love...[or lust] in the brain. This ancient technique is not difficult to master. It only requires eliminating the sensuously defeating proposition that the only real moon is a full moon, and then compensating for this misperception by spending more time looking at, and for, during a new moon, the largest, roundest, most voluptuous object in the evening sky. Note also that the moon is androgynous by preference. You may fill your Yellowmouth with the sexx [gender] identity of your choice. Yellowmouth keeners come in all colors and kinds. Male, female, both, changeable, and in-between are their moon [genders]. Find yours by measuring it against your fantasies and desires. A Yellowmouth Moon is open and transcendent. It will take what you give and return it threefold, often on a cascade of glowing inner warmth. Try one [Yellowmouth Moon] on for pleasure. If it pleases, wear it every time it reappears, and be happy in the union of what is now and has been forever a marriage made in heaven—everybody's moon married to everyone's hope in the universal body of life. Δ

Gulf of Amherst, Burma, November 7, 2001

WICCAN MOON WATER

She was, she said, pregnant with the moon, from a twisted
Tryst on the brink of swift horizons, past the pointed toes
And rocky tops of the Bay of Painted Herons, one sweltering
Summer night, off the coast of Old Rangoon.

On her back she swam under speckled glass in shadow sided
Skies, panting words of penetration through honey dripping
Lips, she pushed her breath to breasts afloat, adding quickness
To her hips. On swells of yellow she called the fellow, keeping
Count of all her tries.

When her lover's gold had held its mold in her whirlpooled
Eyes, she spun herself and trapped his glow in the hollow cup
Of pink between her thighs, then she squeezed him up
Like a prize inside, in one swift and loving dive.

The Poet and the Painter Man mourned the death of yellow
Ocean. The Accountant and the Rajah asked what a stolen
Moon was worth. The Voyeur and the Porno King asked
To photograph the birth. The TV Man with mike in hand
Queried her commotion:

She loved, she said, the silky feel of a moon balloon, spilling
High lit beams and other things in the pit of her comfort sack.
She said as well, in a wink from hell, that she would someday
Put him back, far out of sight, some veinless night, through
The eye of her monsoon.

Interior Borneo, 1935

SULPHUR

Drugged by a dart the night before, Masina found himself emerging into consciousness face down in the center of a clearing. His mouth was dry. His joints ached. His head was throbbing, and a feeble effort to rise shot pain through his wrists and ankles. He had been spread-eagled and staked to the ground. The mid-morning sun was cooking his back. A fire pit next to him was smouldering. He could see from his right eye a stack of blowguns, cut bamboo, and monkey meat in a bowl on the other side of the pit. The fetid perfumed earth of the dark interior was full of the usual screeches, whoops, and whistles—a circus of birds and primates, some of them human. To his left he could see the mossy grey foot of the rock cliffs he had descended yesterday on ropes strung by tribesmen more than a quarter mile up.

Sweat poured in his eyes. His breathing was labored, nostrils flared with the pungent smells of decomposition—the detritus of flowers, vines, animal and fruit carcasses hanging traces in the air. But something was different. The sunlight was hazy, saturated with a yellow tinge, opaque, bitter. Was it smoke from garden fires up the valley? Some hidden volcanic pit bubbling up its own incense? It didn't matter. He lost the thought with a start when several tribesmen slipped into the clearing and began to palaver within a few feet of him. One of them had a peculiar rhythm to his speech. He talked in a kind of gasping pattern, chanting, punctuated by singing and shuffling feet. He called himself Jiwa, spirit or soul. Was he the Malay shaman the villagers called Soul-Eater? He kept referring to the magical *jin* of the earth and wind, paying homage to Nenek the Invisible, cursing the path of the White Monkey. He said he had magic to call down the moon and to hold it at will, as a way of striking fear in the hearts of his enemies and of casting immunity against sickness and death among his own people. He had chosen this day to use it.

M: *I should never have told them that my name is Samoan for moon. What do they want from me? Witness to this ritual? Object of it? How can I escape? I need help. The stench is killing me....*

J: *I will feed Masina's soul to the steam, renew the moon in the birthplace of the moon, remake life. Through fire, water, the smell of the moon in the earth, and the saying of names, I will take control of the power to appear and disappear in the universe, to die and be reborn, to bring the night moon to bear on the events of the day, to be deeply alive, transcendent —soul catcher and dream maker, shaman, yellow of the earth and night....*

Later that day, a great sulphurous fog filled the clearing and Jiwa disappeared. That night there was no moon. Masina, haggard and torn by the ordeal, was set free.

Stonehenge, Wessex Chalklands, July 21, 1997

A GIFT OF THE JOURNEY

Magical megaliths. Stonehenge. Sun mask. Druid dance.
The hand brushes the obelisk—mossy green and grey,
cold for a summer's day—dragging fingertips across
the texture. Braille for a pulse? We want to touch
the mystery of this place, even as the mind's eye squints

for a glimpse of deeper meanings, sequestered in time
and cultural distance, some of which seem to be murmured
in the eclipse of stones at dusk and dawn. But the magic
does not reside in the stones themselves. It is embedded in
the reading, the immersion of self in place, and the puzzle

of the circle that only gets more puzzling when spotted
by the eye of the sun. Like the morning dew, this Druid
magic is tied to a clock of nature. It emerges from nowhere
and disappears just as mysteriously with the heat of midday
—or too much inspection. Poets who would see this clearly

must chase the beams gently, introspectively, as they refract
on the traces of magicians and astronomers who have danced
through the bosom of these stones in patterns and rhythms
we hope are coded within us all. The experience steps us
into another reality and with all the power of ritual turns

day to dream, taking us out of ourselves for a while to show
us something about ourselves—about how we have been
and where we think we used to be—a kind of mythopoeic
archaeology. The best poets still know how to do it. Magic,
it seems, is a gift of the journey.

III. HISTORY IN PIECES

Bruce, Mississippi, January 2, 2001

THE PASSING OF
MONICA HARMON

Bob Dylan called her Maggie
Her daddy called her honey
      Her mother called her sin

They found her up by Sage Creek
Black hair ensnared in ribbons
      Fake diamond on her hand

Her heart had tricked a gypsy
On a bumpy ride to back seats
      Stoked hotter than a kiln

Now her eyes were dark as pockets
On the backside of the moon
      Her lips turned rocky rim

She said all she ever wanted
Was to kick her shoes off, baby,
      And to always be my friend
      —just to be my friend

Hank is a fiction but the incredible story related in "Midnight Swim" *is otherwise true. It comes from an interview with Sergeant Charles C. (Monk) Arndt, my model for Hank and one of three survivors on the mission, as told in* The Old Breed: A History of the First Marine Division in World War II, *by George McMillan (Washington: Infantry Journal Press, 1949, pp. 52-5).* "Letter from Laurie" *forms a counterpoint to Hank's position in the same historical time frame but to virtually nothing else related to his wartime experience except increasing sentimental distance to match the stretch of geography. Staking out a conjunction of such relationships is a structuralist's technique designed to reveal the territory in between. In this case, the sacrifices of war and a classic "Dear John" letter mark territory to be filled in by the reader. Much can be concluded from this mix about the relationships preceding and following the events reported simply on the basis of the reader's familiarity with the problems of war and sentiments experienced with young and uncertain love. That content should track the reader's culture specifically. An old semiotic axiom is that how one interprets experience is a function of who one is—in this case revealed to the reader through another exercise in laconic texts and cultural cuing.*

Guadalcanal, Solomon Islands, August 13, 1942

MIDNIGHT SWIM

Stuck on a sandbar on an inky night,
    A Marine patrol of twenty-six
Crawled up the beach and set a line of protection
    Twenty yards in on the edge of a tangle
Of worrisome jungle
    The colonel and a few men
Eased toward some grass huts
    Hoping to find shelter,
They were surprised by gunshots
    The sand splattered and the colonel was hit
The captain crawled out to him
    Discovered a big hole in the man's face
The man next to them was stabbed with a bayonet
    Hank touched that man's heel
And began to slide backwards
    Then machine guns lit up
And pinned everybody down
    They could smell the powder
Feel the concussion from the muzzles
    Hear the screams as people were hit
The dull thump of metal on flesh
    Without a radio, any chance to use the boat
Or a way to leave by land
    The captain said someone had to go
For reinforcements
    Hank said he could swim for help
At the boat base up the coast
    Naked except for his socks
And the shoes he couldn't untie
    And wearing a helmet with a .45
Locked butt down under the chinstrap
    He snaked into the water

Slipped away from the action
       Made some noise crossing a sandbar
And someone shot at him
       He pulled himself along by hand
On sharp coral patches
       Swam the deeper parts
Rested when he could in the shallows
       Saw a figure moving parallel on the beach
Shot it, heard it thrashing in the bushes
       Continuing to thread along the reef
He found an old canoe
       Half submerged with damaged planks
He dragged it out, dragged himself in
       Paddled it toward the base
Until thirst and cramps and bleeding
       Made him want to quit
But he would look back and see
       The patrol's SOS tracers in the melee
Then go on again, one stroke at a time
       For what seemed an eternity
Finally sentries challenged him for a password
       He didn't know
"Million, million!" he shouted
       And they knew he wasn't Japanese
He was cut deeply from ankles to hips
       His finger bones protruded
They wrapped him in a blanket
       Gave him a phone
Situation urgent! he said to command
       The patrol was being shot to pieces
On the edge of that reef
       On a night of great giving—Send help!
Seasoned men who knew what to expect,
       The patrol fought to the end
Two more escaped before dawn—
       None of the dead were ever found

Sandusky, Ohio, June 13, 1943

LETTER FROM LAURIE

Dear Hank,

*I just got the packet of letters you sent from
Guadalcanal. Mom and I were thrilled. They were
tied up in one bundle and smelled like seawater!
I read the one about doing your laundry on the
old tree that fell in the Lunga River. Bet that
cooled you off, what with the bugs and heat and
all. Dad says you can use orange juice to wash
the smell of gunpowder off your hands. He never
actually did it but it seems to work well for
getting stuff off of his hands from the shop.*

*We were sad to hear about Hugh and Chowdie. War
is so difficult! Please stay well.*

*Bobby and his girlfriend came over last night to
talk about the big game coming up this Friday.
Bobby is going to start at shortstop because
Jason got hurt in a car accident. The sheriff
said Jason was drinking but his dad says that
Jason never touched a drop! Anyway, Jason is
okay and Bobby is getting a chance to play under
the lights. We are all going to the game
together. Wish you could be here.*

*I don't know how to say this without hurting
your feelings, but I'm going to the game with
Jerry Dale, Mary Ann's big brother. I'm so
lonesome. I went out with Jerry once before
(just for a coke) and he makes me think of you
so much. He is so much like you. Strong and
handsome. He has a great job at Valley Wheel and
Bearing and he's fixing up his motorcycle. He
wanted to serve with you and Chowdie but the
Army said that his feet were too flat (something
about his arches, I guess).*

I know we promised to wait for each other. But you've been gone for more than two years. I cry every night. Mom thinks the best thing for me is "get on with my life." She loves you. You know that. But I think she is right. I can't take the sadness anymore. Maybe you should do the same thing, at least until later, until the war is over. The newspaper said most of the First Marine Division was in Melbourne on leave. Maybe you said that in one of the letters we just got. I'll look for it. But to be fair, I'm letting you go on your own. Since I am going out with Jerry, if you want to date an Australian girl, please go ahead. That may be, as Mom says, the "best thing for us."

Well, guess I'll close for now. Be careful. Write when you can. I still love you.

XOXOXO,

Laurie

The history of visitors to islands in the Pacific raises the issue of the poetics of imperialism and the process of translating beings constituted elsewhere into the signs of the receiving culture (see also "The Visitor," *later in this volume).* "The Equation" *draws on the historical record to show that such encounters can go terribly wrong. In the first part of this relationship, a visitor ruptures the island rules governing hospitality—classic Polynesian behavior expressed in this instance through probing conversation and a meal specially prepared for a visitor who refuses to eat out of the categories of his own culture and therefore refuses to honor the reciprocity that contains all such hospitality—at minimum including the obligation to receive and in the long run to reciprocate. In the second part, he pays for his transgression. His rejection is the rejection of an imposing culture and a determination of his place in the Polynesian schema. The following pieces in this sequence,* "Journal Entry" *and* "Bartzholter's Map," *represent different voices and genres of information from other times and places. Discovered fortuitously in the midst of some scholar's archival sweeps, they offer at least two possible conclusions to problems launched in* "The Equation." *The Reverend Fishburne draws on his own culture's myths of colonial superiority and the need to translate Others into the familiar idiom of savagery, on the one hand, and his tapping of the great "lost at sea" myth, on the other. What was from the Polynesian view a colonial offender becomes in the dominant culture of the times a victim, and the cultural turf of the savages is threatened with erasure in the name of God and other aspects of the beholder's culture as a result. Such is the headstone, the epitaph, and the history of cross-cultural collisions everywhere colonial cultures have carried their big sticks. The map—a special kind of text of great interest to historians and mariners alike—rewrites the story in important ways.*

Nukumea Island, Eastern Pacific, March 21, 1869

ISLAND CHAINS

Rinsed in ship colors and the island shadow,
the sea contains us.

Ahead lie miles of tropical green raveled around a giant
sculpture, slow travelers, facing outwards, on a raft of stone.

Flying fish and dolphins show the tops of their water loops
in bow wash that strings out like froth from a fast horse.

Pantomimer clouds puff around a tree line on the peaks
—mouthing clues, looking wild, saying nothing.

Muffled drums thump the air in high valleys.
Hard water shades give way to streaky greens and blues.

Skating on azure glass, the ship slips by grass hatted huts,
coconut mounds, and cooking fires set in short lines.

Tiny figures gesticulate on the beach, gangloading canoes,
waving red cloth and a tattooed sail. Semaphores for what?

Paddling hard from the margins, seaborne sticks and men,
anticipating us as we anticipate them.

Was Mendaña here? Melville? Will escape be necessary?
The Captain readies cannonfire as a precaution.

No one speaks the language. We are prisoners of our own
device, shackled to history.

Links with locks, I think, as the anchor drops.
                                        No keys.

44

Nanafatu Island, Central Pacific, June 17, 1874

THE EQUATION

I.

Sit down with us here next to the candles and the lamps this is my sister and her child Nanafou she is older than my son Fetuu but not as good with a spear eat what you see we have plenty on this island life is strong for us entwined like reef to wave mother to child fish to sea some people have more guns than gods we have no guns our gods our ancestors still live here and speak to us and counsel us when we share tasty fish or snails with them or taro pandanus breadfruit sago crab sometimes mangoes eels and pork the food on your plate go ahead eat your fill it is good for you good for gods why do you resist are you afraid of the blood you must eat this bounty or we will be shamed this is our net for catching good will for smoothing roughness for quieting disharmony for rescuing wayfarers the shipwrecked and the lost a web for living as one in the chain of islands that is our birth and continuation our wind all who come ashore in peace are welcome do you not understand the gift of giving this is our life the fruit of handlines seines and gardens the sap of the tree and you must eat it in honor eat now and wear the flowers of solidarity the shells of beginning my wife is watching you so are the elders and children huddled in the bushes breathe deeply inhale the spirit of the gift the mana and grace the sunsets of this magic creature the turtle we save for chiefs offer to you eat it now eat it all ...

We can talk eat and keep the mosquitoes away with fans you say your dog disappeared in a boating accident mine is still a good sailor where is your tall village do villagers steal land in England do they grow their own food have a smoke take two want some barracuda my mother's brother went to Tabiteuea to weep his son died on a ship they had a dog on that ship I don't think it was yours here is another kind of meat for you bring him the octopus some fermented coconut milk to stir his appetite the whole family is sad over the death of my mother's brother's son very expensive too can we have some money where is your money he hit his head in a storm and just died right there on the deck he didn't drown eat your fish and turtle did your dog drown I can look for him if you ask me we know how to find lost things in the spirit world can you pay me for that where is your money do you like my tattoos how do you like our village my daughter our island we are not afraid to die we only fear the death of our way of living are you a soldier where is your war eat that fish drink the toddy light your smoke we can still talk you must be hungry by now are you sure you need nothing more what is more than nothing you haven't eaten anything what is wrong too tired you say you need sleep you have work to do when the cock crows you'll count coconuts but drink none rebuild the cross on the beach counsel our women on clothing we can give your food to the animals start anew tomorrow.

II.

Wake up *you sack of entrails or I'll thunder your skull as you lay the truth is we killed and ate your bony dog when it washed ashore in the storm we stole your money and your gun last night while you slept we took your bullets and your little book and buried them at sea and you are next you are such an arrogant fool you know nothing this is not a naked smelly place a sea tide of savage darkness the underbelly of your better life it is not odd like me to you or you to me your island is the odd one your paper is odd your mother ashamed of your birth your breath shallow and rank your brow always wet and wrinkled like an unfurled sail on an angry ship your eyes afraid of the noise of the night even your gun shoots the wrong things your war is a hungry whore inside your head who sucks out the spirit of island people and fills you with the ghostly marrow you eat my thoughts gobble my soul but dare not touch my food so here pigface hungry man from a cannibal land here is another plate for your copra company another chance at another gift for your church before you leave you can eat my words my old words my odd words the name of* my *dog the names of my gods you can eat the ceremonies of renewal we shared with you eat the dancing instead of the dancers you might even lick the color off the moon while it sits in the lagoon maybe swallow the islands in my mind these are your foods cannibal man your stomach is as dead as your soul were you born dead are you the living dead nothing is worse than a hungry corpse except perhaps for one that refuses to go away when there is no more blood to drain or that refuses the gift of true life...*

We cannot fill your hunger here you must leave us and know that no island god will have your selfishness no island people will receive you or your stalking plans your hearth has no heart you are death incarnate and you don't know it you must leave us forever this canoe of mine will lead you to the middle sea the home of ferocious spirits eat them *if you can and drink what the sea splashes in your face or pray for rain try to find something to share when no one is there and then eat it all yourself do you think your god will care you take what you want when it is not offered you refuse what is offered when it is different you do not know how to give or receive you do not know what to take or when to take it you are death on a foul wind a slimy red and dangerous whirler you must turn away from us and never look back take the canoe but no coconuts you can feast on the honor you have ripped from us sip from your pantry of stolen virtues and when the sail fails and the sun splits your lips boils your excrement and blinds you to the stars perhaps you will learn to swim in the wake of your own refusals perhaps your righteousness will float you like a hand hewn hull your piggish head point the way to conquerable land before you are yourself conquered and sunk by the weight of your silver cross I am shamed by you the run of your blood in the sea will be my tears drink them as my final gift share them with the fishes the sharks the gods of the sea go now to greet* them get off my island!

Nanafatu Island, Central Pacific, August 5, 1874

JOURNAL ENTRY

Apparently the Holy service of Dutch missionary trader, Mr John Bartzholter, has come to a tortuous end. He seems to have gotten into a squabble over some food with the local chiefs at Nannafahtoo and was mercilessly set adrift in one of their pagan canoes without provisions or sail nearly two months ago. On learning this dreadful news, we searched south by southwest for two days, the direction of the prevailing current that pulls away from here this time of year, and reached the atoll spit Mahnoomahnoo on the morning of the third. Rough seas prevented us from landing but the Captain spotted some wreckage on the north side that could have been the remnants of Mr Bartzholter's canoe. There are no trees so it would be easy to determine if anything was moving about. Discounting a solitary loggerhead that slipped into the brine shortly after our arrival, nothing alive came to our vision despite several hours of circumnavigation and anxious perusal. We did see a partially buried patch of white cloth that might have served as a feeble shelter or a distress flag for some unlucky soul. But the nakedness of the land and our proximity would have made even a corpse easy to see from offshore and none was found. It seems certain that fate delivered Mr Bartzholter elsewhere. Since there is no known land lying in the current between this tiny isle and Nannafahtoo to the north or beyond it to the south for nearly three hundred miles, we have concluded with heavy hearts that Mr Bartzholter was thrown by bitter savagery and injustice into a most cruel deprivation and death on the high seas. May God have mercy on his soul. Not a fitting end for a dedicated man who funded his

Holy mission by serving as a copra broker for the South Seas trading firm of Godeffroy and Son. The rough treatment he received from the natives in these waters over the past several years is indicative of the need for speeding up the work of the Lord wherever darkness prevails. Captain Pennecrest plans to make a full report of Mr Bartzholter's victimization on return to Samoa and to recommend again that these islands be cleansed of their murderous ways. No man, woman, child, or commerce from the civilized world will pass unthreatened by savage heathenism until all of these islands are wrapped securely in the love of Christian destiny. To that end I am and shall remain eternally dedicated.

In Testimony to His Almighty Power,
Your faithful and humble servant,

Rev. Jeremiah Fishburne

American Missionary Society
Honoured Guest, H.M.S. Serpentine

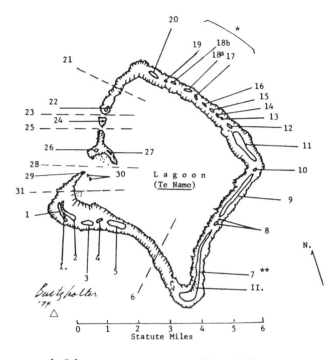

20

19   18b
     18a 17
21   *

22   16
                            15
23   14
24   13
25   12

26   27   11

28   10
29   30   L a g o o n
31   (Te Namo)
1   9

                             8

                        N.
1.
2   7 **
3   4   5   II.
6

Bartgholter '74
△

0   1   2   3   4   5   6
      Statute Miles

1. Fale   17. Teafualoi
2. Savave   18. Matanukulaelae
3. Motuloto   19. Matalaloniu
4. Teafualoto   20. Funaota
5. Motumua   21. Paefa (channel)
6. Teasangaloa (channel)   22. Teafaatule
7. Motulalo   23. Teavafooliki (channel)
8. Motuloa   24. Lauafanga
9. Kongalotolafanga   25. Teavamua (channel)
10. Niualuka   26. Sakaalua
11. Lafanga   27. Teafuaone
12. Niutepu   28. Teavalalo (channel)
13. Niuatui   29. Teafuave
14. Teafuaniua   30. Teafua
15. Niuatali   31. Teaatee (channel)
16. Niualei

I. - Main Village at Savave
II.- Old Village at Motulalo

HUKULIKA ISLAND

Bishop Museum, Honolulu, July 19, 1972

HUKULIKA ISLAND[*]

---

[*] Archivist's note: This was drawn by former missionary trader John Bartzholter, as the notation shows, in September, 1874, while he was a resident of Hukulika Island. It was collected as part of his personal belongings by Captain J.-P. Dumond, of the French trader *Angelique,* on May 5th, 1914, from the local government leader, Chief Peni Tua. Bartzholter had passed away the year before and was buried in a shallow grave near an abandoned village on an islet across the lagoon from the main village. According to Captain Dumond's log, based on conversations with Chief Tua and others, Bartzholter arrived at Hukulika as a castaway in a canoe after having some trouble with the locals at Nanufatu, which lies some 240 miles to the northeast. He was nearly dead of overexposure and starvation when he was found on Hukulika's outer reef early in July, 1874. Captain Dumond was also told that Bartzholter remained on the island from the time of his rescue until his death, never once attempting to leave. He was apparently well adjusted to island life, heavily tattooed, and an accomplished fisherman. He is said to have married a Hukulikan woman after his third year on the island and is survived by several children, some of whom still live there. The Godeffroy trading firm and the American Mission Society, both of whom employed Bartzholter in some capacity before his disappearance at sea, have been notified of these facts and are searching their records for persons to contact in Connecticut, where one of Bartzholter's sisters is reported to be still living.

Hukulika itself was uncharted until the turn of the century. It was spotted at night on December 7th, 1901, by the crew of a Venezuelan freighter, *Cielo Verde,* that had been blown off course in a severe storm. The captain of that vessel, N. Berán, made no mention of seeing Bartzholter, although several of his crew made a reconnaissance of the island and apparently had some intercourse with the local chiefs the following day while they repaired some storm damage inflicted on their main vessel. The island has only one villlage and totals less than two square miles of territory, surrounding a coral reef. Dumond's account is the only known record of Bartzholter's whereabouts since he was set out from Nanufatu. It seems fair to conclude that Bartzholter concealed himself from the few visitors to Hukulika while he was there. He could not have done that without help from the islanders. Why remains a mystery. The map gives no clues. A curious history.

J.M.B.

New Spain, August, 1539

PROEM FOR THE QUEEN OF SPAIN

Your Most Holy Majesty, Esposa to God and the Holy Majesty King of Spain,

I am in the humbleness of the poor servants of this wretched land asking of you to share the Grace and Beauty of Your Holy Motherhood to the publics of Nueva España and to give us Your Love as You would Your Own Children absented from Your Grace by the Mysteries and Wisdoms of His Holy Father. *(Khe San is a malfunction, Sir, like your mother and this whole fucking country!)* We are Love and Truth for You, as You command. The marks on our bodies are God's Will, His Gift to the Wonder of our inhumanity, Glory Be To God, and the brave deeds of the Leadership of the Church and all Soldados in finding us who have been most lost in the Darkness of Satan and the cravings of our flash and blood *(Lui lai, lui lai, you Cong-faced motherfuckers! Back up and nam xuong dat! Nam fuckin' xuong dat! Lie the fuck down! Or y'all gonna fuckin' die sucking full-metal eggs in this goddamn dog-humping ricehole piece of shit you call home! Nam fuckin' xuong dat!)* to be better. We have been blind in our pulque customs and sacrifice of the unforgiven enemies who would join us in keeping the Darkness from the True Light of Your Holy Motherness and saving us *(One more fucking Dink shows his pockmarked little Congolese dick in this bar, we're fucking outta here, and that eye-winking body-bag of a bitch on your lap ain't coming with us.)* from the depths of Hell on Earth. Please do not think of me inexperienced in the Ways of God, Your Holiness, for I am benefitted for years in the Embrace of the Mission and the Love of God, Amen. I am with horses everyday and have learned *(The LT is in the LZ with the VC without no fuckin' radio. What the fuck else could you want for Christmas?)* the Power of Prayers and Writing. The benefits of a Sacred Heart are to love all of God's Children as You love us. Your Majesty may be served in such a way by the humbleness of us and strength of our hands in the land *(Spitshine your own ass, pal! If it don't look like me, walk like me, and talk like me, I shoot it. Simple. Saves time. I fuckin' live. They fuckin' die.)* and the will of our humble publics to assemble as One in the end of civil strife and the junction of all to make gold and fight Satan with *(Hooeee, motherfuckers! Night scope this! Hot stuff for you Mamasans, coming down right now! Brought to you this evening free of charge by Little Nicky's Napalm Factory, Uncle Fuckin' Sam and the Pharoahs, and all the good people of Iowa City, Iowa! Burn, baby, burn!)* the help of Almighty and the generous Mother in Your Love. All a naked man asks is to be Clothed by Your Wisdom, Grace, and Love. Omine Ospentu Dios,

Forever to Your Service, I remain,

Fernando Junípero Dominguez de Ixtapatl
Nueva España, The Year of Our Lord, 1539

"Proem" *is an ethnographically rich and complicated document and I think testimony to the power of laconic texts. Whether or not Fernando Dominguez was as real a person as the historical Jesus Christ, I cannot say. My sources suggest that he was a charismatic Indian from what is now México's northern territory. Apparently he was trained as a translator by Spanish missionaries, made his first trip to Spain in 1537 as a servant in the company of the exhausted and forlorn explorer Cabeza de Vaca, and was returned to México shortly thereafter. His prose/praise poem to the Queen of Spain may have been stimulated by a draft of Cabeza de Vaca's proem to the King of Spain—His Holy, Imperial, Catholic Majesty, Charles I of Spain, Charles V of the Holy Roman Empire— that eventually formed the prologue to de Vaca's account of the ill-fated Narváez expedition to Florida and New Spain from 1528-1536. In any event, the multicultural theme of Dominguez's wobbly statement can be read through contemporary eyes variously as a reminder of the crushing* *power of Empire, the many layers and difficulties of cross-cultural translation, the power of naming, and semiotic diversity in codes. It can also be read as a call for an anthropology and history that include not only the victors but also the vanquished, the paramount and the powerless, the voiced and the voiceless, and the observers themselves. As an erstwhile historical document, it revisits 20th century pleas for a history sensitive to its own ideology; in its passion, divisiveness, heavy gendering, and contrived supplications, it speaks to the need for an empathetic and humanistic anthropology and to much of what exists as subaltern themes in modern criticism. And not least, in what has to be a surprising form of text, it begs the presence of a modern translator's or reader's own culture with its distracting "soldier talk" as fits of profanity and interference from another violent cross-cultural collision, the war in Vietnam. The overall effect puts anthropology and history squarely in the poetic and sometimes hallucinatory world of magical realism, of fantasy and reality mixed in special and compelling ways, in this case specifically in a universe on the order of Gert Hoffman's* Balzac's Horse *(New York: IPC, 1988), Tim O'Brien's* Going After Cacciato *(New York: Broadway, 1978), and* Gunter's Winter *(New York: P. Lang, 2001) by Juan Manuel Marcos. For translations of de Vaca's final text, see* Castaways: The Narrative of Álvar Núñez Cabeza de Vaca, *edited by E. Pupo-Walker and translated by F. M. López-Morillas, Berkeley: University of California Press, 1993, pp. 3-4;* The Account: Álvar Núñez Cabeza de Vaca's Relación, *translated by M. A. Favata and J. B. Fernández, Houston: Arte Público Press, 1993, pp. 28-9.*

The next selection continues the work of texts constructed on an extraordinary premise, and it does so in a comparable place. "Para Donde Vas" *engages time and place with the fictionalized freedom to transcend both. Crossing these boundaries in Méxican geography and history, the passengers fly by towns, territories, and events in limnal time, a perspective of last thoughts that is neither here nor there for the passage but reaches a reality framework that is normally beyond appearance to the living, that is, one that comes from*

> *discovering the specific parameters of your own death. In this case, it frames the gateway to ancient Méxican death—one phase of an endless cycle of renewal and rebirths, propped up by blood sacrifice and the knowledge that "Life had no higher function than to flow into death" (Octavio Paz, The Labyrinth of Solitude, New York: Grove Press, 1985, p. 54). Love of México both calls for the sacrifice and takes you to it, albeit sometimes by strange and unexpected means.*

Border Bar, Vista Clara, México, March 27, 1999.

PARA DONDE VAS

Thick smoke from hand rolled cigarettes
wafted out with words from sweet painted
ladies and the chatter was low and easy.

Bartenders clinked pesos in glasses spread
out like a dime-a-toss carnival game next
to the register and the big neon Tecate para mí.

Mariachi from a fifties box dragged a roomful
of wispy eyes deep through the soul of what
will always be La Isla Encantada, our México.

Swaying to the music, a couple of drunks were
huddling over dice in the corner and swallowing
beer belly shouts about sevens, somebody's sevens.

My fingerprints cut stripes on the sweat of a fresh
bottle as I ordered two more chilled cervezas para
llevar y dos quesadillas con chiles habaneros.

It was 10 o'clock in the morning but no one
knew or cared until the door to the courtyard
unzipped a blinding white hole in the wall.

"Time to go," said the silhouette as we all
squinted in his direction, "if you want the bus
to Oaxaca, Tabasco, Campeche y Quintana Roo."

* * *
* * *

We had taken the bait of deception—walked through it
like rice paper, right on to a moving air conditioned bus.
It was sleek, bigger than a diesel, and many passengers were
already aboard, neat rows of various ages and ancient faces
tinted green by refractions of the sun.

Propelled by a strange rhythm,
perhaps the pulse of indecision,
or a god with an unearthly stride,
we rode on in a collective murmur,
contemplating our purpose of discovery,
casting about for a hint of true self, of knowable
context in this suddenly new but seemingly old lineup
of selves collected in rare circumstance.

The road was smoothed by a whistling cushion of air.
We were startled by the changing sensation
as we began to rise off the ground.

A sense of destiny quickly replaced our sense of destination.
Even the driver had disappeared. But that did not matter,
for we knew by then that the bus was being steered
by our thoughts, by the pictures of México in our minds,
and that we were traveling faster than the dead.

Enthralled and disoriented on the rim of life,
part wounded bull, part conquistador,
my finger traced the northern deserts on a map
retrieved from the seat pocket in front of me,
and Sonora, Chihuahua, and Coahuila
appeared immediately in my window.

Hot land stretched uninterrupted
from one corner of the eye to the other.

A city in Durango pancaked into a twinkling line
on the dusty horizon.
Deer and a cactus made footprints on each other.

Glimpses of Tarahumaran poverty. Spanish silver.
The sun, a gem, a god. Father to fire. Brother to heat.
Antichrist to water.

A child seated in a pan. Alone.

The bus swerved sharply and we dipped into history.

Below, on the ground to the left, Pancho Villa pointed
directions to a train of horses, mules, and gun-laden men.

To Villa's west, the exquisite Doña Baja showed
the apron of surf snugged up to her midsection
by a long rope of highway punctuated in spots
by small fishing villages and men with nets in boats.

La Doña Baja had a heavy footprint, a pointed toe,
dipped in the Pacific. She was crawling with people
and pisces, traps, and aspirations directed outward,
to the blowholes in the bay.

Whales still see the land.
Sometimes they cry for the living, in Spanish.
On this day they lumbered northward,
eyeing their calves, singing to the pod
in patterned clicks and creaks and groans,
oblivious to shorebound desires.

Villa turned south.
He saw another soldier of freedom,
the Indian Emiliano Zapata, riding hard on a snorting white
stallion, leading the prayer trail of beleagured campesinos.

Eager to palaver, to join forces, and driven by angry
memories of Spaniards, landlords, foreign bank accounts,
and countless baskets of peasant blood,
Zapata and Villa galloped into an uneasy alliance.
Gladiators on matched horses, a fiery sword in each hand,
righteous victory in their throats,
they would ride together against rapacious politicos.

Some time and territory passed, snaking right and left,
winding on the map.

Nuevo León, Tamaulipas. San Luis Potosi, Zacatecas,
Sinaloa. Nayarit—your shellfish bay, rising and falling
like the slow, firm, lovebeats of Bucerías. Jalisco, Guanajuato,
Hidalgo, and Michoacán. So much to know, so much
to remember, so much to forget.

Colima, small and joyous, basked at the foot of the Sierra
known as Madre del Sur, La Iglesia de San Felipe de Jesús
punctuating the center, spire pointing knowingly to Heaven.
Go west and you can reach the beach of contented gulls.
You can touch the hand of God if you stay and pray.

Guerrero, we fly by your margins.
You remembered Zapata in 1974,
even as we remember you now.
Godspeed your trip to harmony,
your war for peace.

In the middle was Mexico City.
Aztecs in stone and bone everywhere.
Ancient sacrifice of dripping hearts.
Modern sacrifice of broken hearts.
Diaz Ordáz and his political orgies.
Shadow of the corpse of Porfirio Díaz,
still leaking oppression. El Presidente Portillo,
today marking a cash flow to somewhere unknown,
in invisible ink.

Canals of mercury that run slow with poison,
dripping, ironclad irony. Dead birds.
Puebla. Wrapped in Popocatépetl, Iztaccíhuatl,
Pico de Orizaba, La Malinche. Volcano gods.
They taught you how to cook clay, how to slay the French.
Zaragoza remembered Zapata on the 5th of May.
Signs of the streets and the calendar.
Cinco de Mayo, forever.

The love of brothers, and the smell of napalm
in the morning.

Vera Cruz. Land colors were invented here,
then painted with the first flower colors,
which were lifted one at a time
from the deep color boxes of the seas,
with their rolling white and azure lids.

Your easel moistens our souls.

Oaxaca, clean, like your Virgin of stone.
Zapotecs and Mixtecs, marginalized by your prosperity.
Memories of Aztecs, Olmecs, Totonacs, and Mayans.
Miseries of Spain. Dominican conquests.

Chiapas. Bandanas on Indians, more guns and tears.
The green pounding sounds of mother jungle.
The curanderos and brujas will help you.
Seek peace through the stone wisdom at Palenque,
under the shrouds at Bonampak and Yaxchilán.
Read the water. Read your heart.
All the magic is hidden at Catemaco.
Chango macaques can read the trees.

Tabasco, Campeche, Quintana Roo, the road east.
Talking flowers, birds.

Into Yucatán. No one can resist your splendor.
Your mystery. Mérida, Spanish city, Mayan burials.

Voices thin and distant, drowned by commerce.

A woman bathes her baby in a creek.
Another nearby whispers into folded palms,

"You stopped our river of tears and were ambushed
on the banks of your own, Emiliano. In the morning market,
in the embrace of the setting sun, in the kiss of the sleeping
Jesus, we will remember you, and we will ask the Blessed
Mother to carry us to Truth, to bind us with Freedom
in this hour of our challenge, this drought of hope."

Tears marbled in the dust of lonely roads,
signatures on the parchment of the poor.

Land of contrasts, it said in the brochure.
Ancient priests were there,
spilling blood to keep the universe going.
Spaniards were there,
immortalizing themselves with quill and ink and sword
as the pyramids of the dead repainted themselves red.
Benito Juárez, who knew and drew the blood of the law,
was in there too.

No mention of enshrining love or music drawn
from the marrow of universal life, the charred labyrinth
of indomitable spirits and periodic agony, the fountains
of soul-fed perseverance, or the handmaidens of hope
inscribed on temple walls, announced in temple prayers.

Even the Day of the Dead has promise.

This land, México, the pulse of our loins,
the magnificence of our past, alternately conceals
and reveals beauty beyond imagination.

Peoples deep in time, rich in spirit,
glowing cenotes of emotion, intoxicated with God,
bearing heartbreak and hardship, casting kinships of help,

like nets with flashing eyes, wherever despair darkens
the children of the sun, this golden seed of the circle of life.
Archaeological and political ruins. Blended strength.

What will be your future? What will be your history?,
I asked.

And they all began to sing

¿Adónde vas, querida?
¿Adónde vas, mi vida?
¿Adónde vas? ¿Adónde?
¿Adónde, México mío?

> *Remember Zapata.*
> *Remember Villanito,*
> *Tepoztlán, Xochicalco,*
> *and the life of Benito.*

> *¿Adónde, México mío?*
> *¿Adónde vas, adónde?*

The bus rolled on, upwards, toward the white hot wheel
of the sun, to a black spot (a door?) at the intersection
of Flint Knife Tecpatl, the Serpent Coatl, the Monkey
Ozomatli, and Xochitl the Flower, entrusted this day
to the plans and desires of the Death's Head Miquiztli.

I opened my last bottle and thought of the little girl
bathing in the pan. Alone.

Pesos and oil.

Obsidian butterflies.

And jaguars with emerald teeth.

PLATE 3. *Sunstone.* Watercolor
by Janie Brady, ©1999.

The metaphor that life is a sea voyage is ancient and widespread in human thought. It anchors human life on dry land and sets it at special risk on the sea, marking possibilities and impossibilities for transgression and triumph, opportunities for failure and transcendence—in exploration, commerce, escape from the ordinary and oppression, triumph over natural boundaries and cultural circumscriptions, and extensions of the twin powers of naming and knowing, of making sense of the traversable world. Shipwreck looms in this domain as a dangerous disturbance of prospects, a reminder of human frailty. It is death or dismemberment that lurches from what is ultimately an unfathomable source—a personified sea that alternately seduces with beauty and bounty then steals human life in a moment of inscrutable and, if not unimaginable, at least underestimated force. It crushes the vehicle of engagement on a wet and trackless path, reduces it to debris, and in some unknown rhythm expels its remnants to the land. The passenger who survives such a passage from terrifyingly wet to safely dry is necessarily transformed, internally and in the eyes of society, and becomes an anomaly of sorts, something to be explained, another dimension of challenge to be named and known for future reference. Shipwreck is a sign that the inherent power of the sea cannot ever be mastered by mortals and may be offended by those who try. But punishment for self-assertion is the very stuff that when it fails makes heroes out of survivors and gives rise to cultural braggadocio about vision, courage, and persistence in the turbulence of human existence. This would seem to be especially true among those who extract a living from fickle or unstable environments. Harvesting the sea has heroic dimensions in every culture touched by it. The variable circumstances of fishing, hunting, or scrounging for natural resources in other ways on the open sea can help us or kill us or reduce us to struggling supplicants and let us live to tell the story. The story offered here has no heroic survivors, only voyeurs after the fact, shortly thereafter and in the long run, who see themselves in the spoilage and skeletals of a dangerous world—spectators who understand implicitly the message and the mythics of the wreckage on the beach and

> the triggering dangers of whaling and who try to use that information to decode both the larger enigmas and the pressing realities of the moment. In its metonymic particulars, this is a cautionary tale wrapped in the history of signs of the sea. It becomes a whale story in every sense of the term.

Somewhere off the southern coast of Viti Levu, Fiji

SHIPWRECK

"Sail me not in this place, ye ill fortuned wind,
    In this ship of the damned, ye whalers of fate."

[January 19, 1889]

Squall line turned funnel cloud, dark and heavy on the horizon, gaining strength, fixing on its target of fear, arriving with supernatural speed on an ear splitting blast of sparking air and a cyclopian wall of frothing water, stinging the crew, mastering the captain, as the vessel is picked up, spun high, twisted and slammed, smashed, bowsprit down, across the shoal, foundering for an instant in the deathgrip of demons and thunderous breakers, then capsizing completely in a pounding rage of screams, pleadings, concussions, shredding canvas, snapping masts, splintering decks, and water, water holding, water curling, then whorling and sucking, lifting timbers and terror in a whip of blinding wind and rain, raking agony across ridges, barnacles, and daggers of coral in a chaos of crosschop, a wave from the left, then another, a right higher than the last, furious fists of foam and stone, pummeling, splattering blood and surf, sinking and dragging the wreckage inland, further with every push and shove, every desperate stretch for shore, every grasp for the antithesis of wet, for dry sanctuary, turned ironically this day into sunlit coffin for the cold remains of the maelstrom, this hellish foul wind, horror from the unfiery deep.

[February 21, 1889]

Dust motes swirling in the geometry of sunbeams, piercing the dank shell of the hull, like glintings in the cracks of a passing storm, framed by the rotting planks of a badly gouged name, *Whalerider,* just above a big hole in the side, chest high, a fathom deep and wide. Crawl through it. Ropes and rain diced with sea water in the ribs—air brimming with the uncanny stench of rats and rot, straw, hogs and chickens, whale mold, smothering heat, stove oil, charcoal, rust, fear, and death. Inner timbers split and warped, scrimshawed with the finger scrapes of desperation and confusion—the harried need to hold on to something, and to escape. Flotsam everywhere—ship's papers, a cup, rotting cloth and hammocks, shelving, a parrot cage. Ship's dog, harpooned on a nail high in the hull, now a maggoty slip of bone, hair, and flies. Hardwood transom split in half. Hatches cracked or missing. Masts torn loose, half out of the surf, pointing the way in an unfinished crawl to land.

[January 19, 1989]

Sunny. Hint of breeze. Low sea, green and white winks wrinkling into mild surf, spreading bubbly fingers up the loins of the beach, salting the sea grass, sanding the sand crabs, teasing the dry line, retreating and repeating. Birds muffled into distant peeps. Peaceful day. Pacific. But the splintered wreck on the rim shows how deceptive this sea name can be.

There are ways to ply this salt bourne dame, to seek her counsel and mercy. But beware the captain who finds her placid, or the blaspheming vessel that curses her moods. Even the breathless latitudes of the horse get coarse when ridden the wrong way. Inked by the greedy marriage of foul casts at seabound creatures and too many wishes for faster wind, Neptune's fateful daughter can scuttle your ship, conjure a different ride, run you hard on a ghostly tide—eerie steerage headlong into stabbing reefs and lost beaches by a power hellbent for rest on a rockway where the sea does not span. Infuriated by the whalers' ill harvests on a flesh driven vessel named for its beastly zeal, it was that selfsame placid dame who peeled away their sea, who showed them how many ways a whaling life can mean.

Named wrong by a port with no pride, *Whalerider* made the wrong wishes, ringed the wrong fishes, sought the wrong oil, reached the wrong shore, at the wrong time, with the wrong heart—an emblem of evil entombed in a wreck, and, with another wave of irony, also of hope sprung eternal in King Neptune's court, a tribute to salt justice, a snippet of sea history signed by crossed whalebones, crooked seaward in the sand, leaning, yearning, remembering—she's a whalesong sung on stormy nights, and to newborn calves on their first sunny days.

Branagh's Run Cemetery, Southern Ireland, October 11, 2023

DEAD PAINTING

As sure as I am rooted in glade and glen and perfumed
air, and mindful of the mist in this garden of heartfelt
stones, this toss of chiseled monuments to moments
in the sun, I know that everything dear to me, ever
thought by me, or wished or willed or wrought by me

Will in time pass into particles that glitter with the
pigments of the cosmos. When death brushes me over,
ties corner to center, texture to line, finishes its shadow
stroke on the canvas of love and life that was me and
mine, I will on the instant be drawn into the gallery

Of stars and be spread among them. No longer visible
at the stone of my name, eyes to heaven will find me
daubed on Venus, tinted into lightstreams that color
up Andromeda, the Crab Nebula, Jupiter, and Mars—
an ion cloud mixed forever in the beauty of everything.

IV. SHADES OF SCIENCE

PLATE 4. *Darwin's Reef.* Watercolor
by Janie Brady, ©1999.

Playa de la Muerte, South Pacific, July 4, 1969

THE TIME AT DARWIN'S REEF

From the flatlined stained glass of its church and its crown,
Darwin is jewels all the way down,
A marriage of sea things
and land rings,
Manufactured in time, planted here
on the edges
Of wondrous bright brine,
The sea world of islands, in an ocean of time.

High Time. 1:05 p.m., Fiji time. Ears plugging, cleared
with a quick swallow.

Below,

      Stained glass windows   jewelry of Darwin's Reef

    Glittering treasure

Studded in

    Bits of

      Sand   trees   reef rocks foam sand reef foam
                   scattered across   an indigo sea

Dazzling, inspirational,
breathtaking, truly a priceless gem of timeless beauty.
Well, beautiful, to be sure. But time is everywhere here.

Time to Get Down. Cessna skimming coconut treetops
for what seems a long time.

Dip, bump, skid, brakes, backwash, done. Touchdown.
Limestone runway.

Right on target.

Three hours, 43 minutes air time. Right on time.

+
+
Island Time.
Runs at rock speed.
Born in primal fire on
the ocean floor, Darwin's
core is layers of coral wrapped
around a submerged volcanic peak,
eased upwards in eon increments until
pushed out of wet into air and aquamarine
splendor, crowning its head at the surface with
a necklace of precious corals, stretching to the clouds,
donning a green mantle, mollycoddling birds with insects
and shelter, luxuriating in the clockable eye of the sun,
bathing in the rain, kissing the mist, and winking at centuries
of big moons slipping their horizons. Then, for one deep
reason or another, it began to subside, hanging more paint and
gems on the water line, stringing others out slowly on the way
back down, bridal flowers tossed en route to deepening bliss—
eventually disappearing in the center of the crown, leaving
behind a flat barrier reef, a true coral atoll, weathered and
webbed enough to hold its sand against the easier waves, an
inevitable host to the immigrant holding power of wily scrub
and a gang of sand grabbing coconut trees. Slow time in
a warm clime. Just right for long term coral attachments,
bonds that are bound to stick in time.

$\partial°\approx\approx_{\llcorner,}$ $\qquad$ $\partial\partial°\approx\approx_{\llcorner,}$ $\qquad$ $\partial°\approx\approx_{\llcorner,}$ $\qquad$ $\partial°\approx\approx_{\llcorner,}\partial$

∂°≈≈‿ɔ,　　　∂∂°≈≈‿ɔ,　　　∂°≈≈‿ɔ,　　　∂°≈≈‿ɔ∂

Time Limits and Dreamtime. A barrier reef,
　　Darwin's beauty palette paints a mixed message:
　　　　Begging for transgression, it seduces in waves,
　　　　invites feasting in the windfall of its landfall,
　　　　　　wandering in the wet of its
　　underpinnings,
touching cheeks, bodice, powder, and coiff.

　　Heated by the universal desire to penetrate and be
penetrated, this I am and am not a barrier relationship rises
finally to an animal dance with what appears to be
　　　　rock,
　　　spun out on a reef of dreams,
　　　　　in a time for being,
　　　　　a time for returning
　　　　　　　to the times and tides running silent
　　　　　in our veins
　　　　　　　—to salt, not of the earth,
　　　　　　but of water carried in our
　　　　　fetus sacks and brains, holy water of sorts,
　　　　timeless in composition,
　　　　timed in the cycles of use by each vessel. Our vessels.
　　　　Our time. The time of our lives.

Time for Impersonal Sex. Show time in slow time,
slow growth of coral stems, stars, flowers, brains, antlers,
and aprons, in a slow coming out. It starts with a good moon
and continues
for several evenings, webbing itself in the interim around earth
turns,
tides, currents, and the proximity of sun and moon,
preparing for a slow roll in the bay.

Copy time in the coral (sex by any other name) in one
sense is pure lightning: by geological tickings, corals have
sex in nanoseconds. By the finer grains of the hourglass,
coral joy comes once a year, when the time is right, when

a bright rising moon raises gazes from the depths, warming
water drifts downward as heat for the slaking, lingers
in thermocline, opens the curtain, sends out the news:

Coral is coming.

On cue, tiny biomass blobs, each containing coral sperm
and eggs, ooze out of pores, drift out of hollows, rise
adventurously in the currents,
    seeking attachments, continuation, perpetuity,
    a renewal of beauty
and mass,

$\partial°\approx\approx_{\iota}$ $\partial°\approx\partial°\approx\approx_{\iota}$

$\partial°\approx\approx_{\iota}$ $\partial°\approx\approx_{\iota}$ $\partial°\partial°\approx\approx_{\iota}$ ∂ $\partial°\approx\approx_{\iota}$
    ∂

And all from what seem to be tiny miracles: ejaculating rocks,
busy floating hope around in their sexual best effort to be;
but they are animals all, blossoming shapes in globular capes,
most with plant cells to boot,

ooooöõooooôòóoooo••óooooo•ôòoooooooo
On the slow road to limestone.

High Noon on the Margins. The price for this organic
magnificence is death, sometimes cycled faster than birth,
but always there, lurking, only a plankton eater, smashing
footprint, smothering chemical, trash barrel, or blindly
dropped anchor away—careless moments equal kill time
on the reef. Hard air (not oxygen in liquid) time is also
deadly to corals. The wondrous paints and sparkles of life
seen from the air are thus deceptive in their transformations:
many corals in the uppermost layers
                              are already
          dead.

Space/Time. Residue, remains, raw materials normally pass
from wet to dry in rock time, where sea snails zip by like
so much zenon gas in hyperspace, blurring into light streams
in the rock fixed gazes of nonrocket coral as it creeps in bits
and bundles into the upworld of blitzing storms,
decomposition, and erosion—into the hands of gods
who also have an appetite for sculpture, and who make it,
of course, in their own time.

Magic Time. A chemical time, a time for turning. The margin
of deep to shallow, waterborne to surface held, is a place
of great alchemy: sperm to egg to bone to stone to sand;
first wet, then dry, washed by rain and wind and wave into
gravel, then pebbles, then sand that eventually pyramids
above mean sea level, hauling in seeds shoved ashore
by a generous sea, catching others wrapped in bird juice,
warming up to the probing, circling sun, encouraging
vegetation while hoarding sand against the trades of tossing
seas who rake back against their biggest beachings; in time,
king coconut shows and stakes out more turf, serious help
for hosting more scrub, birds, seeds, plants, trees, and sand
—new jewels in the crown—more reef turned to obstinate grit
and stone, a sharp monument to itself, weathered smoother
as time drips on, enlarged as a field by dropping sea levels
and diminished uplifting in the core.

In the hollows, more slow spooning in the moonlight, more
glue, continued signs of timed continuation, of deep being,
origins, and gardens beyond belief—a hotbed
for the symphony that plays the notes of island life,
pools the rounding dances of corals and peaks in weather
warmth and tidal wines, and sends out the sounds of lifetimes
to all creatures of the air and sea.

∂

Gate Time. We cross a shallow flat of worn coral, blanketed
by anemones, crabs, specks of nursery fish. From the outer
edge, you can see a forever sky pushing down on a placid sea

that eyelines on that trail right back to you, lapping at your
ankles, where, on the edge, just past your toes, colors tail off
from crystal green and aquamarine to indescribable blue.

Time Warp. Sunbounce. Refractions.

Blink in the mirror of these seaside sands,
With air on your back and time on your hands,

> *This wobbling window of Alice glass*
> *Will frame your face and ask you to pass,*

>> *Dive through yourself, your image in wine,*
>> *Into time suspended,*
>> *silent floating time,*
>> *In a jewelstock forest*
>> *full of creatures divine,*

Time Under. In. Sun high and visible through the calm
surface. Thirty feet below, we hover, fly, weightless, silence
diced only by the sound of our breathing and the glub
of bubbles lining up in sunbeams, seeking reunion in the cage
of air overhead. Working seaward along the edges of the wall,
soft corals, fluid and waving in the currrent, hold the face;
most of the hard corals are on shelves landscaped by sea
anemones in succulent colors and shapes.

Seduced by texture and hue, which can signal poison or danger
to fish, humans want to touch. The message comes back
from some with a sting or a stab:

This is food for the eyes, not for the fingers. But the zinger
tends to be tardy. A moment or two of careless touching can
kill twenty years of coral growth.

Heavy lifting in a coral garden
can be a catastrophe—perfect for masochists, though,
since the engagement cuts both ways: coral armor cuts back.
It can hurt and poison and swell you up like a jelly balloon.

It just doesn't come back for a second round in our time.
A fight of different realities. An easy knockout, with no
winners.

Time to Get Deeper. Reef building Anthozoa, working most
unfuriously, are secretly depositing limestone in lines we can't
see—carving, moulding, and populating this sanctuary, giving
algae and other key diminutives a stable place to live. We
meander down through, eastward in the current, to a giant
meadow below.

Shelf Time. Beautiful flower corals. Huge star corals. Smiling
moray. Massive brain corals. Mollusks abound—whelps, tuns,
and cowries. $\partial\partial°\approx$, Fish and mantas, memory prints
hunting a feast of plankton—spawning sets a memorable
table.   Barrel sponges.   Orange and yellow sea fans.
Schooling silver, high and low.   Nature's paint factory.
Giant clams. $°\approx$, Angelfish. $\partial\partial\partial$ Snappers. $\partial°\approx$
More nudibranchs.   Jacks darting. ∂ Jellyfish, smaller ones
chased by a stingproof Hawksbill turtle.   Three large
groupers, grouping. $\partial°\approx\approx$, $\partial°\approx\approx$, Nurse shark,
nursing her lack of speed. $°\approx\approx$, Staggering schools
of rainbow runners everywhere.   More snappers.   A circus
of color, obeying only needs of seed and stomach. $\partial°\approx\approx$,
Stingrays.   Barracuda schooling.   One solitary male
hanging off the edge.   Cuttlefish flashing red, purple,
and brown in fluorescent tones.   Mustard yellow sponges.
$\partial°\approx\approx$, $\approx$,$\partial\partial$ Reef squid, scanning, staring, computing
circumstances and familiarity, competing in intelligence
with the inquisitive octopus, obviously planning
some kind of declaration just below us, in a flush
of shocking pink corals. $\partial\partial°\approx\approx$,$\partial\partial\partial$ More fans. $\approx$
$\partial°\approx\approx$, Parrotfish huddling in bubbles under cracked purple
platforms. $\partial\partial°\approx\approx$, Squadrons of soldierfish $\approx$,$\partial\partial$
and triggerfish.   Electric blue fish. $\partial°\approx\approx$, Single
stingray in a philosophical staredown, inches from my nose,
which is starting to twitch in a sniff for oxygen.

Light Time and Night Time. Divetime in daytime is over. Night time, next time, when light shy comes out prancing, patina surprise rules the color chart, and everything eats or is eaten.

Time to Get Up. Up time is good time, says the body. It will leave without you if you're not careful, bubble up on its own accord in a primal but dangerous inclination to surface mindlessly, quickly. It had to be coaxed with weights and good intentions to get down here in the first place.

Decision Time. Body in check, but thinking fuzzy now, I think. I think. Gorged on coral and creatures the colors of God in water warmer than wombs, even brains can develop a mind of their own. Check watch, gauges, dive tables, aphorism on wrist: *attractions of deep can make you weep.* Trust no one. Everything seduces, especially time. Time to leave. But which way? Don't let the body lead. Make the brain choose wisely.

Read the sign of the times.

Time is up at Darwin's reef. Timelessness is down. Bottom hidden below in blue mist, fading to indigo....

.

....

Baja California, May 16, 1962

DOLPHINS IN THE DESERT

I cannot figure why they change their wet to dry
I will not ever know why they pine so hard to go
Beyond the sweeping deep into deadly Reaper sleep
Past the edge of the sea far removed from the key
    To their own identity

Perhaps it's just because in a world without pause
They need to slip the sharks, the gill nets and barques
Double back on themselves, flee the underworld of shells
And retire with landed man to savannah, bush, and pan
    Where their journey first began

But surely they must know that even freshly driven snow
Has a legion full of trash buried deep inside its ash
That the clearest bluest sky is the biggest kind of lie
Which the naked eye can't see when it's ecoscience free
    Or your pod is out to sea

When dolphins try to steer where the waves disappear
The arid stretch of beach should remain out of reach
Push them back into the sea with an eerie symphony
Let them hear the dying sound of a shipwreck run aground
    They might as well drown

Indian Ocean, Antarctica, January 1, 2000

THE CAGE OF AIR

If the sea is the key to all life known
I cannot say just how it's grown
I only know it started to bloom
With smoke and steam and sweet perfume
From the tropics there in the cage of air

This much is said with hymnal words
That land and sea are blessed by birds
Yet the sloping line of salt and sand
Would seem to be where it all began
At the gateway there in the cage of air

Some came by land and some by sea
To pool whatever they could hope to be
They mixed and mated, and fated and sated
In jellied waves, while the plants awaited
The spores out there in the cage of air

Far ahead of the age of fecund beasts
Plants learned to dance with wetland yeasts
Turning rays and decay into H_2O
To make the whole wide system go
On the bubbles there in the cage of air

Now the sea has fish and sharks renowned
Keeping all with gills from being drowned
But it stops them short upon the beach
When without lungs they try to breech
The dry wall there in the cage of air

With lungs inside, a problem solves
At least for lungers with great resolve
Learning part of the art of deep sea time
They plumb for food in the mighty brine
At the wet wall there in the cage of air

Reclaiming the beach after deep sea reels
Something else obtains in the dance of seals
They caress the sand in a flippered line
Then sniff their share of the seaside wine
From the breezes there in the cage of air

Resurgent life becomes the prize
For cross winged gulls who bless the skies
For creatures stacked and fat with glands
Who find their joy in the high tide sands
Every evening there in the cage of air

Sometimes they meet, these kith and kin
Some with scales, and some with skin
Some with fur, and claws, and tail
Sharing shored up ponds of the seaside ale
From the clouds up there in the cage of air

By now it should be plain to see
This cage has some geography
It's up and down and round with sides
And it floats half full with the evening tides
On the moonbeams there in the cage of air

It's a place where movement has to veer
To its rightful path within the sphere
For a boundary break one cannot bear
No matter what the fateful dare
At the edges there in the cage of air

Monongalis Flats, New Mexico, August 15, 1945

THE SHAPE OF TIME

Longer than a blink, round on wheels of the wagon,
Yet sharp in the splitting of sparked fingers through
The blue haze that swallows the mountains of México
On the horizon of the afternoon, you show yourself
For what you are, for what we know you to be: Impostor.

You stay long in the rivers of song and the night calls
Of coyotes but turn round again in the face of the clock,
Mothers to be, and the spinout spirals of dust devils,
Circling the moment while lovers on the hillside decide
To ride the leaf downwind or to rise as one with the condor.

I have seen you long in jail, short in the hangman's noose,
Masquerading as candy in the child's *piñata*, collapsing
In the charge of the bull, swifting in the matador's sting,
Carving in the browlines of *viejos* and mules, straining
In the tumplines of water bearers and miners in the mine.

I have caught you waiting in the blade of the bandit
And the eye of the panther, slowing on tortoise trails
And the wings of eagles, resting under hats at Matamoros,
Harboring hope in the hidden wet of deep cut arroyos,
Racing on the rails of the Union Pacific and the Santa Fe.

But what shape have you now, in the whisk of prayers
Beneath this cactus cross, in the heat and the haze of God
On this dry lake of life? What shape have you now?
Show yourself for what you are, for what you will be:
Incubator. Healer. Thief. Illusion. The horse of history.

Beth Israel, Boston, November 3, 1999

FRESH WIND
(An Ecology of Breathing)

Rising and falling, riding large cycles
    Returning on waves of air and time
New breath opens itself
    Takes ethereal wing
Whisking outwards, upwards
    In the company of sound
Soars out of newborns
    In a natural celebration
        Of the arrival of now

Not an agony of beginning
    This vibrant coming is a push
Of what were once last gasps
    From other air
Since turned to relocating
    To rising through the underworld
In a noisy salute to birth
    That links before to now
        To then, to used to be

Ties fresh breath to hurricanes
    The jet stream
Horse latitudes of the dead
    Whispers on sibilant lips
The puff of love a rose takes up close
    In admiration
The flow of lung and larynx
    First and final gestures
        And the wind

82

Tallahassee, Florida, August 14, 1986

CANNIBAL-*ISM*

As *"isms"* go

A *Da-Da-ism* is every bit
as good, twice as thick, and often
much more genuine than a
Behavior-ism

A *Surreal-ism* gives no
less intellectual splendor or truth
than even the most robust
Skinner-ism

A *Neolog-ism* is not now
and without artificial insemination
cannot ever be fatter than an
Aphor-ism

An *Anthropolog-ism* is no less
rich in culture than a *Barbar-ism*
or the toothsome grins of an
Anim-ism

But *isms* are the prisms of an
endless, tasteless, organically baseless
and to some much too faceless
Formal-ism

So don't ever catch them. Better
to burn their nests. And for God's sake's
don't eat them!

That's how they reproduce....

Rat Lab, SUNY, Oswego, February 14, 2001

BEHAVIORISM

Maps its rats
    In a lidded box

Measures brains
    To find desire

Eats pastafazul
    With calipers

Sees twitches
    Misses winks

Boils water
    Misses tea

Counts love affairs
    Misses love

Studies darkness
    With the lights on

Sits on me like a rock
    Weighs on my mind

Strapped to my back
    Makes a camel out of me

Humps me like a whale
    When I think about it

I try not to think about it

Recently, nearby.

MEMORY SWEEP

[2:07 A.M.]
Blue juice dams and nerve-lined wires
honeycomb my thoughts while mimesis
soup nectarizes my mind...

    [3:08 A.M.]
    vitamined clocks unlock the gates: vine-like
    sponges cover all terrain; swarming hordes
    of alphabet busters vaporize names, swallow
    numbers, erase frontiers, gerrymander plans,
    and exit coughing...

        [4:09 A.M.]
        ethereal armies pass in dim review
        chanting words that consume themselves

                "Amnesiacs, ... siacs"
                "Amne... Über Alles"
                "Amn..iacs, Amnes..."

[5:10 A.M.]
[sleep now]
[a new day]

[a new dam]
[new soup tomorrow]

V. SELF AND OTHER

Suva, Fiji, February 21, 1982

PORT OF CALL

On the eve of this harbor
    What lights in me?

The carrying sea
    Or the wooden ship?

The journey
    Or the destination?

Tide pools around
    Shoals of desire

Magnificent fog
    Erasable dreams

Albatross omens
    Greeks on the wind

Faces in brine
    Flying canoes

Word stranglers
    On silk veiled shores

Parts traveling each other
    Over bottles of gin

Mind and heart sharing
    The sap of the sea

The sea that lights in me
    On the eve of this harbor

Madrid, Spain, November 10, 1984

RESISTANCE FAILED

Flamenco feet
            furying
Sultry eyes
        glancing
            furying
Then not

Spanish gown
            silking
Ribboned hair
        furling
            silking
Then not

Red and black
            swirling
Birdwings
        beating

In a glass of wine
            swirling
Then not

Let me in

            deep river of song
                cante jondo
            cante jondo

                Let me in

Nukufetau Island, Tuvalu, November 10, 1968

FIELDWORK PASTICHE

Different we are but nonetheless same
Even when appearing to be stuck in between
For I am a you, you are a me, we are a we

Different we are on your shore of two names
One when by sea is the way that you reach
The other by land to the same exact beach

Different we are when you climb up the palm
With high sky desire and a rope on your feet
Or strip off nut covers with very strong teeth

In between when you dance in *fatele* heat
For ancestors I think are plainly not mine
Or at least not the case for a very long time

In between in the muddle of words we share
Three names for chief in your islander slang
Others I bring from my study of Danang

One when you eat cakes from blood of the pig
When you smile and say set out nothing for me
Because you and I know what else it could be

One in our hunger for kinship and feasts
For peppered perfume on the pandanus tree
For tellers of tales that keep us from sleep

One in the blood we shed on coral rock reefs
In the sweat we make with paddles in hand
In the prints we make on sea dampened sand

We are many and one, some this, some that
Not all and not none, a *bricoleur's* dream
Of culture combined sometimes on a seam

United States/México, July 11, 2001

BORDER WORK

Brownsville, Texas, to San Diego, California. One way. Tijuana, Baja, California, to Matamoros, Tamaulipas, plus that extra mileage to the beach on the Gulf of México. The other way. In between are more badges than you can find at an international scout jamboree: state police, local police, county sheriffs, border patrol, agricultural inspectors, INS in more ways than one; if you know how to look or want to find by just causing trouble, ATF, FBI, CIA, EPA, even the IRS; all sorts of Federales, not to mention Policía, subdivided by town and state, some of whom are and some of whom are not self-appointed. Did I mention the National Guard just doing field exercises on land and in the air? Did someone once say to Humphrey Bogart, "Badges? We don't need no stinking badges!"? Where is that man now, when we really need him? Stuck on celluloid in Hollywood. He could be here on the border, patrolling cultures to make sure they stick to each other more, cross freely into the peaks and valleys of each other's lives and lands, and send some badges packing. But he was a bandit. Wanted the gold, all the gold. So he and his compadres would fit right into border traffic and all the legal and illegal commerce that takes place behind the signs and the shanties: gangs for gold, gringos for gold, gold for gangs and gringos, gold for Méxican gringos, gold for American gringos, for Méxicanos, Mestizos, Norteños, and Tex-Mexers; gold turned to happy heads for chicos, chicas, cholo-punks, chopper riders, and low-riders with hairnets; for brokers, truckers, bankers, crankers, hookers, housewives, hackers, and hijackers, all in the chase, swirling around in the giant sucking sound, made not by NAFTA going south, but by the jet powered whoosh of white stuff going north, vacuumed up the collective nostrils of Los Estados Unidos twenty square truckloads at a time. White gold, Mamacita, good shit for breaking through the border of blocking badges, both ways; for helping a throwaway society sniff more to make more to sell more to dump more to sniff more, here and there; for putting yet another foot of poverty and stench on the heap of the Tijuana city dump, already full beyond the canyon where it began; for creating one more need for more badges, more supervisors of badges; for increased patrols between Nogales, Ciudad Juárez, Presidio, and Eagle Pass; for cracking further the cracks in the cultures that built this barbed wire snake of a border between them. But who cares? Cerveza, por favor. Estamos sentado aqui. We're not going anywhere. Show me your badge. I'll show you mine. Let's talk about coyotes. Coyotes never sleep. More beer. The snake cuts but always bends. Me vale madre, joven. My mother loves me. The sun rises in the east. So what? More talk. I hear Tijuana gets hot this time of year. Me vale madre. So what?

Puerto Rico, January 19, 1999

COMBATE BEACH

Placid afternoon, sun glistening on the swells,
painting the beach white.

Cowrie shells, rarer here than elsewhere, wink
their sex in the water ripples; others lie helpless
on the sand—tiny soldierettes who fought
the tides to last night's water mark.

Onshore breeze, gold earring, pirate's treasure
riding a little crest of sand, no doubt dropped
earlier in the day by a strolling cowrie, on parade.

Pelicans and gulls, basking and preening,
file up as fresh life on a spit of rocks stretched against
the grain of wobbling turquoise water—a clutch
of flapping wings, craned necks, and peering eyes
mirrored in sunbeams on the gently undulating glass.

Overhead, an early moon chases the waning sun
at nearly even speeds in the yin yang universe
of rotations and tides—fixed in the wannabe
yo yo motion of marriages strung out with desire
but blocked on the uptake by mimer walls of clear steel,
flagons of hard air, and the rude stiffarm of time.

It is the running trail of the White Rabbits of altitude,
amusing only planet watchers, and Alice.

The bay behind the roll of dunes and beach scrub
grows breezy and green, small whitecaps forming,
spilling on a horseshoe shore lined with seaweed,
the former selves of puffer fish and horseshoe crabs,
and what surely must be Robinson Crusoe's footprints.

Salt pans and an otherwise invisible industry
sit behind the bay—evaporation turned to slave,
seawater hemmed by low walls, easy entry, no exit,
locked in at the mercy of the sun, the transforming sun.

Towering above all is El Faro, the lighthouse,
scanning everything from the upper cliffs,
past the perilous, concave, gaping shelf of red clay,
not visible from the top—an inviting walk
from the lighthouse path on ground that can
crumble into forever on the rocks and surf below.

At the point, off the chain of two small islets,
crossable on the linking reef at low tide,
lies a conjunction of giants—the confluence
of Atlantic and Caribbean waters,
the southwest tip of Puerto Rico.

You can toe dip the water exactly on the margin,
the line of mix, the conjunction of planet juices—
an exchange of gesture for wet inspiration on the edge
of kinship, the roundness, the lip of the sun, sea, sand,
and sky on a round day, looking southwest.

The confluence is capped by a mix of noise to the north,
beachcombers, birds, laughter, music, dancing in the surf,
dining on the yachts, and peace to the south,
the run to the quiet tip, the last inch of earth,
the holy ground of phosphorescent kissing in the tides.

Radical landscapes often inspire descriptions of the predicaments people find in them. Peering over the edge of an abyss is an exercise in interpretation in any case—an attempt to locate significant order, sometimes evil order, in an extraordinary reality of sensations that run from vertigo to euphoria. "Pueblo Canyon" *is an attempt to represent in poetry some of what two cultural traditions that are widely separated in time but clustered in space have made of such things. One tradition shows alienation by experiences in the canyon; the other shows integration by them. A premium on "knowing" in the first instance encourages differentiation, avoidance, and scatology in relationships with the canyon; a premium on "seeing" in the second tradition encourages identity, transcendence, and sacrality in the same geography. The mental appropriations and cultural orderings of the first tradition are anchored symbolically in a fear of falling. Those of the second tradition are anchored in feathered kinship and other forms of bird symbolism. Crossing such boundaries—or better, inhabiting the spaces between them—is fundamental to field experiences in anthropology and to poetics in an anthropological mode. Moreover, as in most cross-cultural problems, the cleavage of Own and Other in the poem is incomplete and ambiguous. On another level of interpretation the very same processes that make the canyon space dangerous also make it sacred in each culture, thereby transcending and combining major particulars of the original divisions. But this lack of closure in the present form need not be troublesome. In anthropology and in poetry we must insist, as Jerome Rothenberg does, that "the work deny itself the last word" lest it foreclose prematurely on the unfolding of understanding, or support unnecessarily the horrendous consequences of the closed mind.* "Pueblo Canyon" *thus enters the hermeneutics of anthropology and poetry as a negotiable item—as conversation rather than pronouncement about ourselves and the problems encountered in relationships with the Others of our frontiers.*

Northern Arizona, June 17, 1963

PUEBLO CANYON

FROM THE OUTSIDE
LOOKING IN

The pueblo's a fortress
Easing out from the clouds
A ruin in craglands
Using shadows for shrouds
Costumed in cold stone
Old bones and fried earth
Its mudcakes and burnt sticks
Signal petrified birth
Its moment is crumpled
Into walls of grey faces
Straight up in a canyon
On the lips of two mesas

White hikers have climbed here
At least part of the way
Ripping landmarks like wildcats
Turned loose on wet clay

They unwrapped their candies
Their guns and their fears
Yodeled tortuous swearwords
Where echoes could hear
Burned an old *Times*
To be sure it was dead
Sprayed tender reminders
On the rocks overhead
Pissed beer on a cactus
And into the wind
Killed off a coyote
And shredded its skin

Turned turtles to prisoners
Of humps on their backs
And got home before sunset
With potsherd filled packs

Their spin in the canyon
Was close to the ground
For they knew that once up
They could only fall down

It is six hundred feet
From the hearth
To rock bottom
—only inches to the edge

High climbers find danger
In this canyon of death
They call it a Reaper
A snuffer of breath

No one can fly it
With feathers tucked in
Least of all humans
In bald bags of skin

Its hallmark is panic
In unwanted flight
Wrapped up with confusion
And screams in the night
Its servants are suicide
Handsome ledges of clay
Vertigo and sacrifice
Rotten ropes with a fray
Its vestments are bloodlines
Ragged out on rock walls
Smashed pigments and red spines
Battered up in the fall

Its pockets hoard skull bones
Near the weather carved floor
Stone jaws caught gaping
In a hunger for more

The sand is not quiet
With any God fearing calm
It pulses with dead things
Every night until dawn

Echoes of ruin makers
Drift up from a sleep
Like cannons in caverns
From a hundred miles deep
Thirsty mad Spaniards
Old fools full of gold
Horsehide and muskets
Stuffed far in a hole

There's a fading of noise
In the thickets of grass
At the end of the canyon
Where the sand turns to glass

FROM THE INSIDE
LOOKING OUT

Twin mountains called sisters
Sit in bright berry time
Wearing aprons of sagebush
Lined with piñon green pine

Below in arroyos
There is corn golden brown
Even sunshine seems planted
Somewhere in the ground

Traversing a rockslide
Fine mist follows dew
Wisping thinly past rooftops
Then dissolving in blue

Birds commence dancing
On cue from the sun
Darting and flitting
Like shots from a gun
They burst past the edges
Catching bugs in midair
Then plunge to the canyon
Eating others down there
Circling and swirling
They rise up again
Grand masters of cycles
That never can end

They often drop feathers
On children at play
Signs of deep kinship
The old folks still say
A kind of communion
In fact is the cant
A common root essence
Preserved in a chant

We are birds of the canyon
Some feathered, some not
Some flyers, some climbers
But all the same lot

Eagles and dreams
Keep the August sky busy
While boys test the edge
And try to get dizzy
They are climbers not flyers
The old woman shouts
But still they keep wondering
How it feels to jump out

By a smokehole at midnight
In the midst of a vision
Kachinas emerge
From a carver's incision
Growing larger in dark
Than they can in the day
Tales of their ventures
Keep the children at bay
Some draw their power
From the magical spruce
While others get potent
From the colour of juice
Decorated with down
From birds of the sky
The carvings hold secrets
About how not to die

Three men in a chain
All ancient diviners
Move quickly and freely
Through the Kiva's vagina
Through bowels and fine pinholes
Changing one size to others
They work out amazements
In the earth of their mothers

Spring maidens spread cornmeal
In crossing white lines
Speaking softly to spirits
About plants of the times
In favor of things
That grow tall in the mind
They also seek plantings
In all maidens inclined

A priest from Black Mesa
Sings a song and a story
About rattles wrapped tightly
And the tortoise as quarry
He is quicker in death
Than ever in life
But the difference is blurred
By the work of a knife
Once captured and hollowed
The shell must get stuffing
From rock salt and magic
And breath from a puffing
When painted with dye
He will always dance faster
When feathered his movements
Will rival a master

Sometimes in winter
Keen ears and striped faces
Huddle up for a songtalk
On distinctive places
On the movement of seasons
And creatures renowned
Through a rolling of timespace
From up world to down
On the unceasing motion
Of earth's great rehearsal
Of forward and backward
And endless reversal
On the birth of breath essence

As unstoppable flow
In hissing red thunder
Near the mountains of snow

There is also great wisdom
The songtalk goes on
In harnessing snakeskins
And in singing at dawn

The beauty of soaring
The songtalk suggests
Often clings better
To those who know best
That birds of the canyon
Have two kinds of sense
One flies, neither dies
And sometimes they fence
So that one becomes other
And abandons its walking
While the opposite creature
Gains the power of talking

But always they meet
These birds of a lot
On the edge of the mesas
Near the land that is not
Knowing when not to fall
And when not to climb

Wearing feathers forever
In the canyons of time

PLATE 5. *Dance Plan.* Watercolor with acrylic
by Janie Brady, ©1999.

Nepotarian Coast, November 4, 1898

BONES OF THE MOON

Hunched by a cast iron wind, by the rust in his legs, by
the mummified bag he drags with some affection, and by
the prospects of his life, the watchman hunts straight down,
claiming flotsam and other trash last touched by the rich
but now stirred and stopped by his ragged feet. Trapped.

Gulls scream and beat the air as he picks the lock and pries
the lid of a discarded vanity box. The intrusion lights up a nest
of pink tissues and sends a cluster of vampire crabs scrambling
through velvet cracks into the sanctuary of his waiting sack.
Changing directions, he lifts a red flare from a clutch of weeds
and probes a packrat hole for more. A driftwood stash gives up
two cups of dried kelp and the track odds from Tuesday's news.
Four crumpled butts smoulder defiantly in a poke in the rocks.
Another hugs the tide with a hiss. A kiss.

He presses on, sometimes waiting and listening, then culling
and filling, always exclaiming and demurring to himself over
this piece or that, until the chill on his face, the weight of his
pack, and the rippled orange of the closing horizon force him
up the side of a dune for the nightly calling of the power.
Exhaling a curse, he squats on his heels, dumps and sorts
his bundle, scrapes a match against a scraggly flint, then
tosses the tinderbark and snot of his throwaway world into
the smouldering pile. The ancient magic of breath and prayer
makes it fire. Manmade hole in the darkness. Crab stew.

Sparks mothing up from the flames to his beard are chuffed
into ashes by the hack of his cough and the fog of his aching
heart. Like a bruise with wings, his gilded shadow skirts
the shore and dances dangerously for a moment in the scan
of a wandering stomach. But he doesn't care. The warmth
of his harvest plants the sun in his knees and the pile itself

seems as high as the rising moon. Yellowmouth moon. Black
robe. Diamonds.

The heat of the fire drags from him a dream of iced whiskey
and dolphins catapaulting through foam in the bay. The sting
of saltwater on sunburned thighs flickers through his mind. He
remembers the smell of the oil of summer women, how he slept
with it for weeks, and how he rested naked on the grass passing
time pasting images of cut flowers and virgin wheat on the baked
blue canvas of a midday sky. Solitude.

That same day the sun cast its eye on an early moon. Rising
like a lover awakened too soon from a long afternoon nap,
having shed her gown, the moon peeked over the windowsill
of earth and gazed back at husband sun, white skin slowly
giving way to the glowing amber of desire, fully committed
now, eager to take her place in the center of the evening,
dappling the sea, lighting the shore. Enamorada.

The vision collapses into muffled ears and sore eyes
as a November wave hammers the anvil of a nearby slope,
covering his cheeks with a blanket of spray and shrinking
the margins of his escape. He awakens reluctantly with a shiver.
Reforming his weight in the sand, he palms the last embers
of the fire, turns his tattered back to the sea, and waits
for the sweep of deeper water. Midnight.

The raft of thoughts returns, steered by memories of alchemy:
water turns moonbeams to bone. The old man dove for them
in his youth. Tugged them up through aching ears. Took them
to the circle of stones. Gave them to the sun. Sacrifice. Unity.

On this night he will swim to the bones of the yellowmouth
moon. He has watched it ease up in solitary splendor, gold
splashed into slivers at the far edge of the sea. He has watched
it go home. Alone. Time and again. He will go to his moon—
swim to the beams become bones, sculptured by time and tide

into arms of the siren, waiting, beckoning, in the womb darkened depths. He will swim to the spiral of life, this incubator, sanctuary, grave of the night, wedding bed of the moon; to coral bones—white as the sun's seed, spilled phosphorescent in water gripping moonglow, in heat, in fiery crystal light, then settling in the sea, finding moon, cooling to shimmering yellow, blue, green. Bones, whispering in the mist, the surf...

> *Ride the numbing tide, moonman.*
> *Ride the gold cascade. Ride it now.*
> *Yellowmouth moon is calling you home.*

Upper Xingu River, Brazil,
April 13, 1934

THE VISITOR

Khaki man
From a paper land

So odd in water
Much worse in dirt

Hugging your Bible
Afraid to work

You were either
Born dead

Or not at all

What do you know
Of Alligator
Honeybee
Jaguar
Anteater
Anaconda
Cappybarra
Or Monkeymen
Who howl at the moon?

Let us smoke on it

Read the swirls
Of your awakening

Jalapeño Wharf, Venezuela, December 31, 1989

WATERFRONT DREAM

*Harbor glow and a distant beacon
slip the black into night fog blue.
Bar neon, flashing red, splashes rouge
in a rhythm on your cheek, blushing,
igniting the mist, shaping your face,
your resoluteness, the impulse
to dance with electric flesh
on the edge of stirred water.*

*Drizzle born breeze tips your breasts,
tosses your hair in an airy passion,
frantic to penetrate the hot hum
of desire that webs your eyes,
streaks purple across your thighs
and the wetness of this sailor's alley,
coloring us like cuttlefish
in the thickening sea of our embrace.*

*Knock of boats, creaking ropes,
black water lapping at my brain,
rising with the taste of smoke,
licking at your lips, your redness,
the fire plumping in cupped hands,
the perfume drip on your skin.
Fireflies lift us in white neon swirls,
spill me, flood you into sparkles.*

*We crackle in the dampness, glisten,
molten figures welded to cobblestone,
cigarette hung faces propped on a wall,
smolders flicking in a funky blue haze
of love and sweat that fades as memory
in the dimming beat of a samba song
and the glare of last call lights
from the oyster bar.*

VI. SEMIOTICA

USMCRD, San Diego, August 27, 1958

TATTOO

Fletcher Christian
Got his in Polynesia.
Where it really
Counts. A necklace
And spirals
On his back.
Island signs for
Feasting,
Fishing for love,
And sacrifice victims.

Yours is nipple high
On your breast.
Where it really
Counts. Two roses
On a stem,
With thorns.
Ready signs for
Feasting,
Fishing for love,
And sacrifice victims.

Joshua Tree, California, April 10, 2004

MOJAVE CODES

Can lead you through a weather wall on a dry lake
Sunshine on the left—grainy rain on the right
While blue skies & a breeze take hard semantic turns
Over muddy mirrors in washes dotted with pools
& wildflowers, out in acres after yesterday's rain
Make sweetness signs for the nose and the eyes

In the distance a chalky ridge points to heaven
Revealing its source of what cannot be snow
Off to the west a buffalo herd of volcanic rocks
Runs a rainbow figure into an apron of dirt
& waves of heat vapor rise from the salt flat
Telegraphing the event to clouds and birds

Semicolons crawl through bony sockets at my feet
Busy in a bighorn skull long empty of sheep
Another critter moved in & died before ants came
& unwrapped the meaning of moisture in flesh
Below them is an ungrammatical pothole
& a cactus bud about to thank the rain

Jackrabbit, a tortoise, joshua trees on the plateau
Fabulous fixings for mesquite tea talk and dreams
Nested in bottle caps & cans & other culture markers
Dried out & preserved like sheep and cattle skulls
Commercials for Twenty Mule Team Borax soap
& Frankie Laine songs about wild geese

Desert texts can make you remember Hansel
& Gretel, heat stroke & a horse with no name
They can satisfy your thirst for knowledge
& make you late for the dance of the dead
They can make you sing, especially after a rain
You just have to give them time

Bora Bora, French Polynesia, September 6, 1972

TAHITIAN FLOWER

wild orchid   moon blush
sunsets and steam

island life   veins
in your pinkness

lingers in   exquisite reds
dusted yellows

painted fingers   close on
delicate whites

desire   blossoms
in your center

spreads   your   wings

insinuates passion

drips aroma

like candlewax
on tissue

on the
thin veil
of my smoulderings

Let me lie in
your garden

Breathe
your ether

Touch
your silk

Soar in
your dust

Bathe in
your raindrops

Drain
your nectar

Drown in
your intoxicants

You are my heroin

my ecstasy

my addiction

my completion

Pacific Ocean, 22°S, 180°W, May 1, 1938

TRAMP STEAMER

Several weeks creeping north to Fiji, the point of my scheduled disembarkment. My rough calculations had us now east by northeast, dead on for Tonga, not more than a day ahead. The captain said two, maybe three, he would let me know. Other stops to off-load cargo? No, straight into port at Nukualofa. Why the change of direction? Why so long? When would I get to Suva? No answer beyond a shrugging gesture that suggested he had made the decision and it was his alone. My plans would unfold accordingly or not at all. He shut the door and left me staring at it on deck.

Maybe it was the captain.

Caracas. Name of the ship and the port of its registry. It had the usual: a greasy hull, smoke blowing black as coal from the fire down below, the stench of coconut oil and kerosene that made the occasional passenger stay upwind of it and on deck as much as possible. Through the glass I could see charts and other navigation equipment strewn about a large table, empty coffee cups, a pistol.

Maybe it was the ship.

South American crew. Wandering the world. No other identities. Stained T-shirts and ragged pants or shorts. Always smoking on deck. Talking in a low hush as they carried out their duties, eyes averted to avoid contact unless I asked a question. Then only one would face me directly and say lo siento, we are no sure, please see el capitán.

Maybe it was the crew.

Maybe it was the baggage. Salt streaks on your trunk, haggard leather straps, antique red smeared by abundant seas, too many carriers. Maybe it was the cotton dress, luxuriating in its proximity to you, soaking you in color. That laugh from deep inside, bubbling up in a pack of chuckling demons. Lips emblazoned with the texture of fine wet silk. Your drink, clinking against the rail as the ship lurched on a short swell or two. The ring on your finger. That cigarette.

Maybe it was you.

Nukuhiva, Marquesas Islands, 1675

FESTIVAL [For Greg Dening]

Haka'iki and *tau'a,* chief and warrior priest
You of so much uncollected fruit, so many conquests
We honor the songs of your ancestors, your *mana*
The *atua* gods before you, the *atua* to follow

We honor *atua* with these *heana Teii*
Enemy men taken from *Teii* for sacrifice this day
Take them to the *me'ae,* the sacrifice ground
Crush them twice, kill them and kill them again
Hang them like fish on hooks
                    They will invigorate, honor us
                    Replenish and restore, honor us

Spirits of the sky, rock, sea, wind, and tree
Sky, rock, sea, wind, and tree
                    Spirits of the sky, rock, sea, wind, and tree
                    Sky, rock, sea, wind, and tree

                    Hear us, we sing to you, dance this story
                    Hear us, we sing to you, dance this story

Spirits of *te vaka* canoe, *Tua to Ha* breadfruit wind
Te vaka, Tua to Ha i Mataiki, Ua, Ko-mui

Spirits of *ehi* coconuts, *meika* plantains, *tao* taro, *ika* fish
Ehi, meika, tao, ika, e ika

Spirits of *matta puovu* lean-faced old men
Huepo black-faced men, tattooed warriors
Matta puovu, huepo

                    Spirits of *Enata* the men, *Te Henua* the land
                    Enata, Te Henua

                    Hear us, we sing to you, dance this story
                    Hear us, we sing to you, dance this story

Mann's Chinese Theater, Los Angeles, November 8, 1957

NOSFERATU RISING

i.

Pale in the dawn, more corpse than corpuscle,
vampyr, strigoi, the gaze of a winter tree, lonely
and enervated on the hillside, fixed unblinking
on the fallen leaves beneath it, branches of long
pointed nails, the eerieness of eternal life sapped
by the rising sun, we fear your enigma, your life
out of chime, here and not here, dead but not gone,
turning touch into terror, taste into honey slicked
up on bare veins, sight into peerings of the hungriest
wolves, smell into blood maps sniffed out of the air.

ii.

Stalking dusks of our suns in your coffin of thought,
you signal your prey from windows gone dark,
whispering the lie that death is itself enrapturing
song, voluptuous experience on the edges of breath,
not really decay crosshatched in a kiss, for old
that grows young with the bounties of flesh,
for makers and keepers of time out of synch,
the worst of all hailers in the tarpits of death,
condemned for all time to share in this feast,
this seductive ascension of harm laced with lust.

iii.

But for your wet dreams you rise dry with the night,
silhouette slicing at the ring of the moon, cursing
snow for its color, its purity and light, life for its
brightness and bastions of truth, you call minions
to follow your howling from hell, declaring
and swearing on the chill of Novembers
that nothing will change, not now and not ever,
for you are still Nosferatu, disquieter of hearts,
arch prince of wounding, thirst quencher of death,
bloodroot and king of all evil in the evil undead.

Regarding the recent passing of friends Marea Teski and Toni Flores, the ever-gentle Miles Richardson said to me that it was enough to "make you want to stand and shake a fist." I agree. Death enrages and defeats. Sometimes it inspires retaliation. "Killing Death [That Bastard's Been Here Again]" *engages death in a poetic mode properly called romantic irony. Its absurdity is therefore licensed. The ethnographic setting in this case is an Irish pub. It's very easy to find someone in a classic Irish pub who will talk about anything, if not someone who is an expert on everything. Smooth and influential talk—Blarney—is common in such settings. Sometimes deceitful, it is seldom pure malarkey. Blarney draws its mark in fact from a sacred stone. And the best Blarney-talk always contains a bittersweet truth. In this case, a recent passing creates great sadness and raises the ancient and perennial prospect of giving personified death a dose of its own project—of defeating death by killing it. The magic weapon is language. Talking is balm for the survivor's grief and it protects others from more of the same, even as it chokes the life out of death itself.*

"My Friend Henry" *is a more conventional lament about the passing of the interconnections of people and places that define the times of our lives, that give us personal history.* "St. Patrick's Day" *continues this elegiac theme and speaks from the grave to a lover about the greens of life and pining for them in the withering erasures of death—the need for remembering what once was in celebrations of the heart on a very green day.* "Show Me a Sign" *gasps at the enormity of death run amuck and yet finds something wonderfully unkilled in the wreckage: a personal expression of solidarity, the deeply motivated need to continue life and limb, and the prospects for doing so in a world more united, more conscious of its interpersonal commonalities.* "Torn Shawl" *is a glimpse of what was lost in other terms and places, no less tragic in consequence to the individuals involved than the World Trade Towers, Pennsylvania, and Pentagon murders, and perhaps an empathetic measure of the particular stories of the thousands of victims from so many cultures and places that fell to earth in fire on that fateful September day.* "Pipers" *is a query of the innocent about death and its music, a*

> *refrain assembled from a parade of symbols a week later that marks both past and future in a stew of heightened consciousness. Should we have seen it coming? Among many other defining moments in our past, the uncommon horrors of World War I thickened the intellectual air on the Left Bank with questions of history and the nature of being human. That's a form of anthropology we contemplate regularly: "Who are we? Where do we come from? Where are we going from here?" Deep ideas. The trick is to put them into practice in a way that promotes unity and cheats death, not the other way around.*

Boston, Massachusetts, August 15, 1998

KILLING DEATH [THAT BASTARD'S BEEN HERE AGAIN]

[hushed, deliberate speech, leaning over table] *Death, you say. Another sad-timing rip up the gullet. Let me let you in on something. A few of my pubmates at the Purple Shamrock know that I have myself tried to **kill** Death many times. I've cursed and spat upon him...*[sips beer, waves barkeep to table for fresh round]*...worried him in my dreams. Starved him by doing healthy and holy things. He seems unfightable, too big to fight. But he has to be fought. There can be no caching of arms on the premise that Death is just the rolling over of life. That's a lying cover for a hunger the likes of which no mortal man ever sees until it's too late. You'll do well to keep your guard up and your aim straight. And never shoot at the heart. **This greedy Bastard has no center!** He is without purpose or plan, save three: Eat what is loved. Nip viciously at the spirit of every caring thing nearby. Strike at night if possible.*

[louder, engaging nearby patrons] **Yeah, Death is cruel and cold and,** *as we know* [sips beer], **unrelenting.** *But there is a secret that has come to some of the Irish through the backwinds and corridors of family lore. It's an idea as old as thought itself— older than shamans, it may be the first magic, and it can set the Bastard on his heels.* [sips beer, points forefinger in air] **Death,** *we have come to learn, is afraid of words!* And he doesn't care much for music either. *Death rots with every song sung at him and just the hint of wit in the room can sting him in the eyes. It works out to be about a pound of words for a pound of the Devil's flesh.* [quiet laughter] *Truly now, the right words, danced out, can really give him a knock. And if you need to slow him down, a song sung true in the light of the moon can lock the Hellion in ice for a week or more. You can add an extra day to his freeze for each really good song and dance performed immediately thereafter.*

So if the truth be known, wordsmithing smites the Reaper and saves our souls. [sips beer] *That's why we talk in our sleep. Why we wrap our babies in poems in the evening and sing all night for the dearly departed. Why our heroes have always been talkers and writers and such. Why we shout on the battlefield and etch the names of the dead on stones and walls and speak of them often. Why the Holy Word is our castle, comfort, and emblem. Why poets are Saviors and speaking ill of the dead is absolutely forbidden. Why the wake is a mighty sop for talking through tears—a festival of toasting, a solidarity of words.* **We have reason to be heard!** [shakes fist in the air, takes long draught]

So tell everyone you know that that Bastard's been here again. *Tell them twice. Then sing it to them and tell them to pass it on. Maybe we can talk the Reaper Thief into his own grave. Maybe we can kill him with what he knows least and therefore cannot resist. Maybe we can kill him with* **meaning born of heartache**....[finishes beer, wipes lips with wrist, bangs glass on the table]

[hushed voice, leans into the table again] *More on this next time we meet.* [louder] **Barkeep?** [waves hand, cuts arc in the air with forefinger] *Another round for my friends here. Another round for everybody.* **Another round for everybody except that sneaky Reaper Bastard hanging in the bushes outside**....

Oswego, New York, February 19, 1999

MY FRIEND HENRY

Take hope and make sail, he said. There is another beach
out there—maybe even as good as the one we combed
that summer in Hawaii on a pledge to drink one tall Foster's
per mile. We fudged. More lagers per mile—in fact, very
few miles overall, many lagers. But it was a good trek full

of laughter and more serious talk about island peoples and
how to learn from them. Dipped in the ancient chemistry
of friendship, ours was a special bond that comes from
the very marrow of sociability and lodges itself as living
text in others through the mutuality of shared experience,

good times and bad. Having it eases heartaches. But too
many hopes for too long have shown that reverie won't
cure heartaches, especially when they are caused by the loss
of a friend. Cancer ripped Henry's sails, put him ashore,
and made him fight. He looked for a counterattack to send

it back to the dank and grievous pit from whence it came.
But he knew that the battle was big and would not be won
easily in the short run, or at all if demonic bad luck took
the early rounds. As it happened, the cell stalker's heaviest
toll didn't show until the middle rounds. And it didn't get

everything at the bell. Mindlessly pounding away at life's
understructure, cancer couldn't find Henry's gift for this rainy
day—the memorable text that those of us who knew him
retain in the sanctuary of the heart. That is comfort and buoy
for us in the wake of a great loss. We'll take it with us and do

some miles for him this summer in Hawaii, or perhaps
at Henry's beaches: Tabiteuea. Tarawa, Nonouti, or Arorae
—wherever the sea keeps its promise to redeposit what
the beach once had. We'll comb the surf and push our canoes
to the horizon. We'll watch for him. And we will remember.

O'Houlihan's Bar, Boston, March 17, 2000

ST. PATRICK'S DAY

Green me. Let me be green. Grow me like grass.
Seed me green in the sea grass green of the sea
of green grass. Let my yellow pool your blue,
slosh into green with you in ever greening rings,
until we are greener than the evergreens
in the lowing veins of the grainy green valleys
of the rolling green hills of the Emerald Isle
on a sparkling green Irish day. Let us be
green together as our thoughts turn green,
new thoughts, minty green thoughts of seedling
green love, soaked in green springs, Spring love,
virgin bed green, innocent green, in neon green
beer spilled on green shirts and leprechaun
pants, lifted in song in a language so green it
strikes a green tear in all who hear, jigs an Irish
rhythm to the twiggy green fife and green
plumming drums of the Chieftains, and tips
a bowler hat from a green excuse me vat
from Bowling Green as it wafts through the
hazy green crowd boxed in green by the green
on the walls, the floors, and in the gullets
of very green men draped in verdant green ladies
on this greenest of all green days. Green my
spleen with another beer of green, my greening
queen, my greenish queen of green. Slick green
me green, shiny green fresh rain in the jungle
green, spot my green spots green with bigger
green spots, green on green buried in green.
Dull green me green, scrub my shiny green
to shamrock green, shine me green again,
buff me, make me lie down in green pastures,
then walk my hills in a long green veil.

Story me. Seed me with tales of the greenest
lovers in the greenest counties in all of Ireland.
Aquamarine, blue-green, pea green, almost
green, forest green. You are these greens,
a lick of leafy green, lime, and the whole list
of greens that go with the greens, fresh as
a green apple and twice as pure, pure green,
wrapped in the sunny green of a dewy green
day that paints the grass of green into even
greener glass. I want to be your deepest green
of greens, your greenest of green marines,
green in your green while you are still green.
So soak up another green beer, my greening
griever, another green beer for the green in me,
the green in you and the green in everybody
who wants to be green, is now, or forever
will be green. I need to be green with you,
green of greens green, green to the marrow.
Green my eyes green, green my hands green,
camouflage me, hide my face in a war of greens,
glow in the dark green, night scope green,
ghostly green, green thread in the funeral linen
green, green dream green. Pour it in green boots
and walk it into me, green my soul. Shoot me
with a green bullet. Green me deeply green,
green to the roots green, arterial green, waving
in the grass, snipping off the bud, chlorophyl
dripping, jungle plant slashing, bleed me 'till
I'm green green that is really green. St. Patrick's
Day green, for example. The green on my grave,
for example. Helicopter green. Vietnam green.
Grassy knoll green.

Oswego, New York, October 5, 2001

SHOW ME A SIGN

There is hope in believing that the bottom line of human nature is ultimately one of sociability, not social pathology. We know that resource sharing contracts in scope with prolonged deprivation and that human relationships which might be maintained in less troubled times tend to get sloughed off under such conditions. Accordion like, the overall pattern includes and excludes people and groups variously in expanding and contracting ranges of cooperation and solidarity, and it is driven by perceptions of relative resource advantage, if not by an interest in survival itself. We've seen this kind of movement in fine grain in our villages and towns and in relations between nations as private interests and political economies slip from good to bad, rich to poor, and back again. We've also seen a reaction to changing environmental circumstances that seeks to expand against cultural difference in wars of ideological and territorial aggrandizement, all of which are fueled by intolerance by definition. But what does this say about us as a species? About our prospects for living up to the name "human" in the process of managing our relations with others? Looking a little closer at ourselves under extreme conditions can provide some answers. What happens in the individual extreme, when all the strategic resource chips are down, when people know in their deprivations that they are past the point of no return, when they believe that they have no chance of resurrecting a life path that would sustain them? There is evidence to suggest that what happens is not a Hobbesian war of all against all, every man (and woman) for himself in an all out grasp for the last bread crumbs, as fearful folklore and under-informed social science would have it. In the end we are social animals.

We know that the grisly facts revealed to the liberators of Auschwitz and other concentration camps at the end of World War II included human beings gassed to death in ovens— victims of hate and cruelty beyond any sense of credibility. We also know that some of them climbed on each other's backs in an effort to escape the confines of their murderous smotherings and that some of them clawed hard enough on the walls to embed their fingernails in the concrete. But that wasn't the end of it. At some point resignation to their horrible fate set in and a sign emerged, a generalizable item, I think, a symbol of triumph of the human spirit drawn out of the psyche in desperation and left for us like a text to be read in a twisted pile of dead men, women, and children. Many chose to die in a final physical embrace, entwining family and strangers alike. I take that as poignant and enduring evidence that we *can* matter to each other, irrespective of who we are, even (or especially) under the direst of circumstances. The ultimate concerns of life transcend what separates us as cultures, combine us in one big mirror image as a species. We could find this thought and organize it in our societies if only we knew how to look—if only we had words to impose the idea indelibly upon ourselves, to remember it in images that flare eternally in the conversations we have about others and differences, particularly when troubled times circle us up around the bonfires of our lives.

Much of the prospect for knowing or acting on this larger sense of humanity is lost to consciousness in the ordinary run of cultures and competitions for space, food, and the certainties that meaningful and satisfying lives must conform to the values of your own cultural beliefs. That's the balance point of life today and there is nothing in our current global repertoire of behaviors and persuasions to keep that pattern from devolving into dangerously competitive relationships, as we saw on September 11th in the viciously culture-bound attacks on New York City and the Pentagon—a fireball of hate and anger exploded in the face of trust. America showed another side of self-interest as it moved to embrace its own in the wake of this tragedy and began to build a levee of heroic strength, high risk relief, and soothing words to stem the tide of outrage and tears. Although retracted in scope from a global perspective and mostly unrecognized in the wrenching national pain of the moment, the prospect for global humanity known and cherished was insinuated in that resurrected solidarity. The blow knocked the wind out of most of the world. The pain was human, not just American, and thoughts of commonalities were showing up in word and gesture everywhere, including ground zero. Some unlucky souls in the tower attacks realized that they were trapped above blazing holes of concrete, steel, airplane fuel and annihilating smudge and smoke that blocked all passages of escape. They chose to jump to a certain death rather than face a terrifying immolation. Hope for the species flickered again briefly in a tiny sign on the way down. Some of the jumpers were holding hands. I don't know what you call that in anthropology. I don't know how to teach its deeper meaning to terrorists or the Taliban. I only know that it has to be said and that we have reason to hear it, all of us.

Isle of Man, September 11, 2001

TORN SHAWL

Shawl of yours
Knitted vee
Draped over a chill
Love scented in wool
Clambering on rocks
Uphill from the sea

Hand of yours
Redemption
Soft touches smoothing
Shredded commitments
Shared shivers of fear
Until healing's begun

Heart of yours
Hearth aglow
Palms fanning embers
Honey mead plumbed
Nourishment drained
Straight into my soul

Flesh of yours
Moist perfume
Red orchids unfolding
Rapture and rhythm
Rising bright as the sun
On splayed winter dunes

Death of yours
Blackened stone
Hard ink on my compass
Dark blood in my brain
Heart weavings rendered
On seabeds of bone

New York City, September 18, 2001

PIPERS

Dear Grandfather,

We saw the parade today

The men wore plaid skirts
Like our school uniforms

They marched in small steps

      Step   Step   Step

All in a row

      Step   Step   Step

The music didn't breathe
It just kept coming out

High notes and low
High and low again

      Amaaazing grace
      How sweet the sound...

      Step   Step   Step

Many people were crying

The pipers acted like they were doing
What they always did when people were sad

I will never forget them

I wonder if I will ever see them again

                    Love,

                        Marianne

Left Bank, Paris,
February 14, 1929

DEEP IDEAS

Ship of Thought
On a Sartrean Sea
|
its nets
have caught
eternity

Δ

PLACE LIST

Abaiang Island, February 14, 1840
Amazon Basin, November 10, 1997
Baja California, May 16, 1962
Beth Israel, Boston, November 3, 1999
Bishop Museum, Honolulu, July 19, 1972
Bora Bora, French Polynesia, September 6, 1972
Border Bar, Vista Clara, México, March 27, 1967
Boston, Massachusetts, August 15, 1998
Branagh's Run Cemetery, Southern Ireland, October 11, 2023
Bruce, Mississippi, January 2, 2001
Cattermaller Swamp, Louisiana, April 13, 1941
Chichén Itzá, Yucatán Peninsula, June 24, 884 A.D.
Chichén Itzá, Yucatán Peninsula, June 24, 1904
Dorothyville, Kansas, September 9, 1999
Fa'apoto Island, March 21, 1799
Fa'apoto Island, March 21, 1899
Fountain Hills, Arizona, June 9, 2001
Funafuti Island, Tuvalu, October 12, 1492
Guadalcanal, Solomon Islands, August 13, 1942
Gulf of Amherst, Burma, November 7, 2001
Gulf of California, July 14, 1952
Indian Ocean, Antarctica, January 1, 2000
Interior Borneo, 1935
Isle of Man, September 11, 2001
Jalapeño Wharf, Venezuela, December 31, 1989
Joshua Tree, California, April 10, 2004
Left Bank, Paris, February 14, 1929
Madrid, Spain, November 10, 1984
Mann's Chinese Theater, Los Angeles, November 8, 1957
Monongalis Flats, New Mexico, August 15, 1945
Mosquito Coast, Lower Amazon, July 31, 1924
Museum of Wicca, Salem Massachusetts, September 23, 2099
Nanafatu Island, Central Pacific, June 17, 1874
Nanafatu Island, Central Pacific, August 5, 1874
Nantucket Island, Massachusetts, July 4, 1999
Nanumea Island, Central Pacific, September 6, 1842
Nepotarian Coast, November 4, 1898
New Spain, August, 1539
New York City, September 18, 2001
Northern Arizona, June 17, 1963
Northern Slope, Mount Kilimanjaro, November 3, 1999

Nukumea Island, Eastern Pacific, March 21, 1869
Nukufetau Island, Tuvalu, November 10, 1968
Nukuhiva, Marquesas Islands, 1675
O'Houlihan's Bar, Boston, March 17, 2000
Oswego, New York, February 19, 1999
Oswego, New York, October 5, 2001
Pacific Ocean, 22°S, 180°W, May 1, 1938
Playa de la Muerte, South Pacific, July 4, 1969
Puerto Rico, January 14, 1998
Puerto Rico, January 19, 1999
Rat Lab, SUNY, Oswego, February 14, 2001
Sandusky, Ohio, June 13, 1943
Somewhere South of Viti Levu, Fiji, January 19, 1889
Somewhere South of Viti Levu, Fiji, February 21, 1889
Somewhere South of Viti Levu, Fiji, January 19, 1989
Stonehenge, Wessex Chalklands, July 21, 1997
Suva, Fiji, February 21, 1982
Tallahasse, Florida, August 14, 1986
United States/México, July 11, 2001
Upper Xingu River, Brazil, April 13, 1934
USMCRD, San Diego, California, August 27, 1958

DATE LIST

Chichén Itzá, Yucatán Peninsula, June 24, 884 A.D.
Funafuti Island, Tuvalu, October 12, 1492
New Spain, August, 1539
Nukuhiva, Marquesas Islands, 1675
Fa'apoto Island, March 21, 1799
Abaiang Island, February 14, 1840
Nanumea Island, Central Pacific, September 6, 1842
Nukumea Island, Eastern Pacific, March 21, 1869
Nanafatu Island, Central Pacific, June 17, 1874
Nanafatu Island, Central Pacific, August 5, 1874
Somewhere South of Viti Levu, Fiji, January 19, 1889
Nepotarian Coast, November 4, 1898
Somewhere South of Viti Levu, Fiji, February 21, 1889
Fa'apoto Island, March 21, 1899
Chichén Itzá, Yucatán Peninsula, June 24, 1904
Mosquito Coast, Lower Amazon, July 31, 1924
Left Bank, Paris, February 14, 1929
Upper Xingu River, Brazil, April 13, 1934
Interior Borneo, 1935
Pacific Ocean, 22°S, 180°W, May 1, 1938
Cattermaller Swamp, Louisiana, April 13, 1941
Guadalcanal, Solomon Islands, August 13, 1942
Sandusky, Ohio, June 13, 1943
Monongalis Flats, New Mexico, August 15, 1945
Gulf of California, July 14, 1952
Mann's Chinese Theater, Los Angeles, November 8, 1957
USMCRD, San Diego, California, August 27, 1958
Baja California, May 16, 1962
Northern Arizona, June 17, 1963
Border Bar, Vista Clara, México, March 27, 1967
Nukufetau Island, Tuvalu, November 10, 1968
Playa de la Muerte, South Pacific, July 4, 1969
Bishop Museum, Honolulu, July 19, 1972
Bora Bora, French Polynesia, September 6, 1972
Suva, Fiji, February 21, 1982
Madrid, Spain, November 10, 1984
Tallahasse, Florida, August 14, 1986
Somewhere South of Viti Levu, Fiji, January 19, 1989
Jalapeño Wharf, Venezuela, December 31, 1989
Amazon Basin, November 10, 1997
Stonehenge, Wessex Chalklands, July 21, 1997

Puerto Rico, January 14, 1998
Boston, Massachusetts, August 15, 1998
Puerto Rico, January 19, 1999
Oswego, New York, February 19, 1999
Nantucket Island, Massachusetts, July 4, 1999
Dorothyville, Kansas, September 9, 1999
Beth Israel, Boston, November 3, 1999
Northern Slope, Mount Kilimanjaro, November 3, 1999
Indian Ocean, Antarctica, January 1, 2000
O'Houlihan's Bar, Boston, March 17, 2000
Rat Lab, SUNY, Oswego, February 14, 2001
Fountain Hills, Arizona, June 9, 2001
Bruce, Mississippi, January 2, 2001
United States/México, July 11, 2001
Isle of Man, September 11, 2001
New York City, September 18, 2001
Oswego, New York, October 5, 2001
Gulf of Amherst, Burma, November 7, 2001
Joshua Tree, California, April 10, 2004
Branagh's Run Cemetery, Southern Ireland, October 11, 2023
Museum of Wicca, Salem, Massachusetts, September 23, 2099

PRAISE FOR *THE TIME AT DARWIN'S REEF*

"With *The Time at Darwin's Reef*, anthropologist and poet, Ivan Brady, has joined the lineage of earlier anthropologist-poets who date, at the very least, from Ruth Benedict, Margaret Mead, and Edward Sapir. The finest moments in these pages are gripping poetic narratives that combine the love of language with a story that takes us beyond ourselves. In these works anthropological poetics is not only alive, but given inspired impetus toward the future."

—Dan Rose, Professor Emeritus of Anthropology, University of Pennsylvania

"The Time at Darwin's Reef is a graceful play of history, ethnography, and poetry that shows us the strange in the everyday and the familiar in the exotic, reflecting upon the thickness of the human endeavor without burdening the reader with pronouncements. It remains open even as it seeks coherence, a measure of a mature mind that has made its travels among us but is also poised for the future. The beautiful watercolors join the search in their own poetry of bright and dark, surface and depth."

—Miles Richardson, Doris Z. Stone Professor in Latin American Studies, Louisiana State University

"What an anthropologist experiences and learns can have many audiences, can take many forms. In *The Time at Darwin's Reef* Ivan Brady invites us to share with him ways in which a range of places and kinds of knowledge can feed imagination, and imagination find novel forms in which to be expressed. The ways in which people use language are part of their culture. Here Brady explores ways in which language, as lines, relations among lines, can be used and varied as part of our culture as anthropologists. These uses of words are descriptive, reflective, admonishing, wondering, humorous, inventive, and varied in place and time. In short, an exemplar of poetry as a verbal tool of ethnography, wide-ranging there, as it is in life, and in this work, truly impressive, with something of the same spirit and flair as Pound and Williams."

—Dell Hymes, Professor Emeritus of English and Anthropology, University of Virginia

"One intriguing irony in Pacific writing today is that much of the best poetry is crafted by Pacific Islanders while most of the bad prose is composed by Western academics—each group describing the Pacific in its own ways. Ivan Brady's *The Time at Darwin's Reef* brings out the best that lies implicit in these different but mutually reinforcing perspectives, embodying subtleties of the region as only poetry, pictures, and 'talk story' can. This is a sensitive and in many capacities brilliant accounting of what can be perceived in the borderlands between sea and land, in the Pacific and on the islands of life in other places."

—Robert Borofsky, Professor of Anthropology, Hawaii Pacific University

"Lyrical, pensive, reflective, and witty in the right places, *The Time at Darwin's Reef* is a highly innovative concept in cultural studies and anthropological texts; through poetic explorations in the times and spaces of journeying for research and other purposes, it clears its own scholarly path to knowing the cultures of self and others. Ivan Brady's fieldwork, teaching experience, and thoughtful probings of substance and style make him the perfect author for such a book. Janie Brady's paintings are imaginative, provocative, and resonate with the text— another reminder that there are many yet to be discovered paths that lead to deeper understanding of cultures and peoples, including ourselves."

—Lola Romanucci-Ross, Professor, Department of Family and Preventive Medicine & Department of Anthropology, University of California, San Diego.

"As good and compelling as many of the individual pieces that make up this collection are, I am most impressed by the way it both unfolds and achieves coherence as a work of anthropology. Here a skillful poetics of text-making builds context as certain and as powerfully as any classic ethnography, while yet being a virtuoso performance of all of those tendencies in the aftermath of the 1980s 'Writing Culture' critique that have come to define the preoccupations of anthropology."

—George E. Marcus, Professor and Chair, Department of Anthropology, Rice University

ABOUT THE AUTHOR

Ivan Brady is Distinguished Teaching Professor and Chair of Anthropology at the State University of New York at Oswego. A former President of the Society for Humanistic Anthropology and Book Review Editor of the *American Anthropologist,* his special interests include Méxican and Pacific Islands ethnography, ethnopoetics, semiotics, and the philosophy of science. He is the editor or co-editor of several books, the author of dozens of chapters, articles, and reviews, and is currently developing a new version of his book on *Anthropological Poetics* (1991). His poetry has appeared in various books and journals, including *Reflections: The Anthropological Muse* (edited by Iain Prattis, 1985), *The American Tradition in Qualitative Research* (edited by Norman K. Denzin and Yvonna Lincoln, 2001), the *Neuroanthropology Network Newsletter, Anthropology and Humanism (Quarterly), drunken boat: online journal of the arts, Pendulum, Cultural Studies* ⇔ *Critical Methodologies,* and *Qualitative Inquiry.*

ABOUT THE ARTIST

Janie Brady's interest in art by and about Native Americans is long standing. Creating underwater art is one of her more recent endeavors and the results are quickly gaining an audience. Her primary medium is watercolors, but she has exhibited other work in pencil and ink. She has traveled extensively in México, the Caribbean, the Pacific Islands, and the American Southwest, painting impressions throughout.